Sarah's Story

BY
GINNY HATHORN

Xulon Press

Copyright © 2014 by Ginny Hathorn

Sarah's Story
by Ginny Hathorn

Printed in the United States of America

ISBN 9781629522982

All rights reserved solely by the author. The author guarantees all contents are original and do not infringe upon the legal rights of any other person or work. No part of this book may be reproduced in any form without the permission of the author. The views expressed in this book are not necessarily those of the publisher.

Unless otherwise indicated, Bible quotations are taken from the King James Version of the Bible - *Public Domain*.

www.xulonpress.com

Thank You

I want to thank Anna Walthall, my dear friend who painstakingly helped me with the rewrite. She is my Rachael and my friend. I couldn't have done this without her wise insights and truthfulness. I also want to thank my family, especially, Dave, my husband, who believed in me and encouraged me throughout the whole process. And I want to thank all my friends who read my book and gave me their comments.

Preface

I did not write this book to deal with the issue of rape or teen pregnancy but to show how life can be lived when you choose to let God guide you. Sarah chose to walk in the "promise land" which is a term I use to mean walking in the spirit. When the children of Israel left Egypt, they celebrated the Passover which represented salvation, and crossed the Red Sea, which represents baptism. God gave them the law, but before Moses could even get it down the mountain, the Israelites had broken the law and fallen into sin. God's plan was to lead them straight into the promise land, but their unbelief kept them in the wilderness. They could only see the obstacles and forgot the power of the God they served, who had done tremendous miracles to get them where they were. Instead of going into the promise land, they were sentenced to forty years of wandering in the wilderness. God still led them and did things for them like providing manna every day, quail, fresh water, and shoes that didn't wear out. But, they were still a wandering people. It took that generation to die out and a new younger generation who hadn't gotten used to the way God moved, who weren't burned by unanswered prayers to go into the promised land. Joshua positioned himself to believe God was still the God of the miraculous and would do what He promised he would do. He was the one

God chose to lead this new company of warriors into the land of milk and honey. It was a land where God would give them every piece of land their feet walked on, houses they didn't build, vineyards they didn't plant...the land of blessings. Sarah dared to walk in this realm. She chose to rise above the prejudices of the church and believe in a supernatural God who works all things for good, who orders our steps, who answers before we ask. She chose not to be the saved who walk around this life with little power, and their hearts full of unbelief. Her story might seem a little far-fetched, but maybe not. God is raising up a generation of Joshua's people who will live in the promise land and live a spirit-led life of forgiveness, joy and the miraculous. You can live this life also. You can be the divine appointment the world is needing to meet. The power of God is living in you and wants to do miraculous things through you. My prayer is that Sarah's life will inspire you to dare to live in the promise land.

Forward

By Anna Osborne Walthall

She couldn't have known anything about me because I was new in town, just having moved from several states away. I was cynical toward people and didn't have much faith in God, but when the sweet looking lady walked up to me and said she had a message from God, just for me, I gave a polite smile and said okay. With that, she began reading from the book of Isaiah "You shall weep no more: He will surely be gracious to you at the sound of your cry; As soon as he hears it, he answers you. And though the Lord give you the bread of adversity, and the water of affliction, yet your Teacher will not hide himself anymore, but your eyes shall see your Teacher" I burst into tears. Plenty of people knew of my adversity and affliction because I'd been through something horrible enough to make the 6:00 news! But not a living soul knew the secret desire of my heart that this lady had just named. It's peculiar, but I have always wanted a teacher. I'd quietly searched for many years, and finally added it to a rather large pile of dashed dreams. But in an instant, as this woman spoke, I gained clarity. I had not been alone. God is real, and He cares about every tiny detail of my life. My defenses dropped, and I wanted more.

Sarah's Story

It turned out the lady was also new to town and lived near my house. We went for cokes at the drive-thru and shared about our lives. We continued to hang out together even though I was extremely eccentric by all measures, and she was a complete enigma to me. When she encountered a problem, whether mine, hers, or anybody else's, she stopped whatever she was doing and took the problem to the Lord in prayer. She didn't worry, complain or gossip, and she laughed…a lot. I watched her closely and asked questions when I didn't understand or trust her positive attitudes and kind behavior. Without taking offense, she repeatedly explained that Christ was the cause for her hope and joy. I slowly began to trust that she was genuine and that she truly loved me. As she continued to credit God with good things that happened, I began to recognize His goodness myself. Because she'd ask me so many times to pray with her for the good of seemingly random people she encountered during the day, I came to believe the principal of divine appointment. She continually displayed absolute trust that God was always at work for her good, and consequently, I grew to trust Him, too.

That sweet looking lady is Ginny Hathorn and she's been my best friend for several years. Through our friendship I learned how to have a real relationship with Jesus…to walk daily with Him…to be in constant fellowship with Him. In retrospect, it's obvious that not only was Ginny the one who delivered God's promise to me of a teacher, but she was the actual teacher He provided. Only God could do that!! I believe if you are reading this, it's because God wants to use the same sweet looking lady and a fictional representation of two real friends to speak with you.

1

Sarah sat in the first hour class of her new school listening to the teacher's first day speech, when she felt her stomach turn over. She was going to throw up...soon. She didn't have time to ask permission; she got up and ran for the bathroom that she had searched out before class for this very reason. She barely made it in time to hurl in the pot. After losing the entire contents of her stomach, she sat sweating on the floor, wiping her forehead with a damp paper towel. Sarah had moved to Monroe, Louisiana, just a month before and knew no one.

That morning she had read Psalms 3 and related to David, who felt like all his enemies had risen up against him. She definitely felt her demons of insecurity, fear, and rejection swarming around her. *Lord, you promised to be a shield around me, and deliver me. Please do that for me today.* She wondered how she was going to reenter her classroom with any respect, when the door suddenly opened and in walked a cute girl who looked vaguely familiar. She looked at Sarah, "Ms. Tanner wanted me to see if you were okay. Are you sick?"

"Pregnant." That was not exactly what Sarah meant to say, or how she wanted it to come out, but it did, and there was nothing she could do about it now.

Sarah's Story

The brown-haired, green-eyed girl looked at Sarah with surprise that suddenly turned into a sly grin. She looked pleased, like she had just found out the password to the school's computer. "Are you coming back to class?"

"Yes, I'll be there in a minute."

Why didn't I ask her not to tell anyone just yet? Probably because it wouldn't do any good.

Sarah went back to class, and just as she supposed by the looks she got, her new "friend" had shared her secret with the whole class. The teacher even looked at her with judgmental eyes. The only thing she could do was to find her seat and sit. Somehow she survived till the bell rang. The rest of the day was just as bad. They say bad news travels like wildfire, and by the end of the day her bad news had blazed out of control. *I guess they have never seen a seventeen-year-old pregnant girl. God, please help me carry this cross.*

Sarah couldn't wait to get home. Every day seemed like "hump" day because it was a feat just to get through. Her house was her retreat. It was a large two-story mansion on the bayou. Built three years ago, it had been unoccupied most of that time, so it was practically new. The view out Sarah's upstairs window was peaceful and picturesque with the bayou and the woods behind it. She loved to sit in her window seat, just breathing in God's handiwork. She spent many hours there reading and thinking...and praying.

She loved to decorate and needed to do something to her new room, she just hadn't felt up to it. It was definitely on her "To Do" list.

Sarah had been a spiritual leader at her church in Dallas. She was genuinely kind to everybody and had many friends. She had beautiful silky blonde hair that had a hint of body and natural curl on the ends. She wore it down and simple. Her blue eyes were the color of a swimming pool that were innocent and perceptive all at the same time. In spite of her thin frame, she was stronger than she looked in every way.

Sarah's Story

She was very athletic, and loved basketball and gymnastics. Good grades had come easy for Sarah who was extremely bright. Sarah had everything going for her...up until now. All her assets could not compensate for her pregnancy.

Wednesday rolled around which usually meant church. Sarah was in her room thinking about how she missed her mom who always made sure they went to church when they lived in Dallas. Sarah and her dad had tried to go to church several times in her absence, but just couldn't seem to be able to make it out the door. They had decided that this would be the week they didn't let their thoughts of what was missing keep them home. They were going to try out the First Baptist Church, which reportedly had a good youth group.

Do I dare go? Sarah got her answer as her dad called to her from downstairs, "Sarah, honey, are you ready for church?"

"Dad, do I have to go? It's going to be just like school. No one will talk to me, and I'll sit by myself feeling like the social reject."

"Where is my strong girl who loves a challenge? How are you going to be Jesus to them if you hide out in your room?"

"Well, Jesus wasn't seventeen and pregnant."

"No, but he *was* born illegitimately, misunderstood his whole life, and crucified at thirty-three by the very people he came to save."

"I know Daddy, and I know you're right. You sound just like my counselor. It's kind of hard when they have already labeled you the harlot," Sarah sighed. "Okay, I'll go...and pray someone talks to me," Sarah said, surrendering to her new lot in life.

"There's my girl," her dad said with a supportive smile. "I know this is hard, Sarah, but we'll never heal sitting in this house feeling sorry for ourselves."

Sarah's Story

"Now, give your dad a hug." As he was hugging his daughter, he added, "I'm nervous about going to church without your mom, too. So I know how you're feeling."

2

They were quiet as they drove the already too familiar trek down highway 165 to church. Even though they lived out of the city limits it only took five minutes to get back in and another twelve to get to church. Sarah had been so preoccupied with her own insecurities and her own battles that she had forgotten that her dad was struggling with his new life, too. Kathy, his wife and her mom, had been killed in an automobile accident a month after they moved there and they were both still pretty numb. They were both just going through the motions of living, putting one foot in front of the other. Sundays had been particularly hard since it reminded them of Kathy, so they had been staying home, watching a service on TV. They both knew they needed to find a church.

Sarah's dad, Corbin Levine, was a very wealthy entrepreneur. He had moved to Monroe, Louisiana to start a new business with several of his college friends who lived there. Corbin's relationship with the Lord had grown much deeper since Kathy's death. Kathy had always been the stronger Christian before.

In spite of their bulging bank account, the Levine's had remained a very humble family. Corbin and Kathy had raised Sarah to value the true riches of the kingdom more than any riches the world had to give. By the way they lived, it was not obvious that they were multimillionaires. Corbin was a great giver into the kingdom, which was one of the secrets to his success.

Corbin already had a connection with the pastor of the First Baptist Church. When tragedy struck and Kathy was taken, Corbin felt suddenly alone in a new city. Pastor Michael McCormick had gone out of his way to be a friend. He had been the one to perform Kathy's funeral. Pastor McCormick called Corbin regularly since then to check on him. Corbin planned to take the pastor to lunch and asked Sarah if she minded if they discussed her situation. She readily agreed. She knew her dad needed a friend also.

They pulled up into the parking lot. The youth met in a separate building called "The Point". Sarah saw the building marked "The Point" so she headed toward it. Even though it was a much smaller building than the rest of the buildings belonging to the church, it looked like a huge tower of doom to Sarah. She found herself secretly hoping the door would be locked or jammed shut and she would have an excuse to go sit with her dad in the service for adults. She also hoped that there wouldn't be anyone there from her school so she could develop some relationships before she dropped the bomb that she was pregnant.

When she walked in, the worship band was already playing. She didn't know that the youth service started 30 minutes before church. That was fine with her. The lights were low and she could easily slip in unnoticed on the back row. Sarah loved worship. She felt alone in God's presence, so she lifted her hands and praised her God and Savior. It felt so good to be in the presence of God and draw strength from corporate worship. She didn't open her eyes once. She didn't care if she was the only person there really worshiping—she needed this.

When everyone was finally sitting down, Sarah looked out over the crowd. There were over a hundred teens there.

She felt a little intimidated, but was trying to be strong. She could feel stares from the ones sitting around her. She figured they were wondering who the new girl was. She was hoping, that was all they were thinking.

That night the youth pastor, Caleb Greiner, spoke on Gideon. Gideon, he explained, felt the least qualified to lead his people against the Midianites. Nevertheless, God called him, confirmed the call, and equipped him to win. *Lord, is that what you are doing with me, calling me to be a leader? A leader of what? Who is going to follow me anywhere? There is no way I'm going to be voted president of anything unless it was President of the High School Moms of Monroe Club.* Sarah almost laughed out loud. *Okay, Lord if you are serious about me being a leader I guess I'll do that but, I certainly feel the most unqualified, and I need a sign from You that I'm going to make it through this, much less be a victorious leader."*

When he finished speaking, Caleb made his way straight to Sarah, introduced himself, and welcomed her. Sarah appreciated that and relaxed a little. He introduced her to several of the people standing close-by. Sarah was gaining confidence until she looked around and noticed one familiar person...the girl from the bathroom. *God not her. Why does she have to go to this church?*

Sarah felt the Lord's reassurance. She knew she could trust God. The girl was already talking with a group of kids and looking her way. Sarah wanted to disappear into thin air. She knew what they were saying, but just in case she wanted some confirmation, a guy walked up and said, "Welcome to our youth group. Aren't you the girl who is pregnant?"

"Yeah, that would be me," Sarah said, hoping to at least get a smile.

"I'm Sarah," she said bravely.

"Oh yeah, sorry, I'm Aiden."

"So, are you going to keep the baby?"

What a boy question!

"I'm not going to abort it, if that's what you're asking."

Who is this rude guy?

He didn't know what to say after that, so they both stood there awkwardly waiting for the ceiling to fall down on them. Sarah eventually excused herself, walked over to the water fountain, and got some water even though she wasn't thirsty.

The girl she had met that morning in the bathroom walked up and asked her how she was liking school. "Met any friends yet?" Sarah could tell the girl was trying to rub in the fact that she had ruined any chance of Sarah doing so.

As Sarah searched for an answer, the girl added, "By the way... I'm Jessica," smiling smugly over her shoulder as she walked toward the door.

What a backstabber! Doesn't she know the Bible says, "Love covers a multitude of sin." She definitely isn't covering me—she exposed me to everybody. Sarah started to sarcastically thank her for exposing her sin but decided that was not the way to be Jesus to this Pharisee, so she kept her mouth shut.

Sarah wondered if this was what her mother was talking about when she taught her to turn the other cheek when being persecuted. Sarah only knew that she had never faced this kind of rejection before. Where was her mother to help her through this? *God, please help me know what to do. I really want to glorify you in this, I just don't know how. I need Your strength.*

While Sarah was trying to recover from these two encounters, a tall attractive teen with dark brown hair, olive skin and striking blue eyes walked up and said with confidence:

"Hey! You just moved here from Dallas, didn't you?"

Sarah somehow managed to answer. "Um...Yes.... Yes, I did."

Who is this gorgeous guy talking to me? Sarah hated that she was so shy around guys, especially good-looking ones.
"What's your name?"
"Oh, uh...it's Sarah." *Does he know about me?*
"I'm Jonathan. We go to the same school."
He knows! Now she wondered why he was taking the initiative to talk to her.

Maybe he was being nice to her because he thought she was a bad girl, or maybe he felt sorry for her; either way, Sarah suddenly felt the need to leave. She excused herself and went to find her father. Meeting a friend would have to come another night. Her dad was waiting outside, and Sarah wondered if his night had been as difficult.

Corbin asked her if she liked the youth meeting. She lied and said, "Yes, it was fine." Corbin knew better, but decided not to press. She would talk when she was ready, and he needed to process some things himself.

Sarah asked him how he liked church. "The sermon was good. I'm having lunch with Pastor Michael this Tuesday. He seems to be genuine."

The next day started out the same way as the first: total isolation, no one to sit with at lunch, no one to walk with in the halls, and no one to talk to until just before her last class, Biology. As Sarah was walking down the hall, she heard someone call her name.

"Sarah."

She turned to see Jonathan smiling from ear to ear and coming through the throng to see her. *What was she going to say to this strikingly handsome guy?*

"Hi!" Jonathan boomed out.
"Hi." Sarah said with less enthusiasm.
"How is your day going?"
"I've had better."
"I know what you mean. Thanks for coming to youth group last night, I hope you come back."

Well, that sounded more like a confession. "Thanks, I'll see...I mean, I probably will." Why was she so awkward, and why did he unnerve her so? She turned and walked into the wrong class. *Arrrggg!!!*

After school, everyone went to their activities. Sarah went home. Normally, she would have gone to the gym to practice layups, or out to the track for a run, but since she was the center of bad attention and pregnant, she decided to go home to exercise.

That night her dad wanted to talk. She was right about his church experience. It had been hard on him, too. Going to church without Kathy was painful, but he did have a moment of comic relief. A divorcee in the church tried to hit on him. That was a new thing for him, and one that caught him totally off guard. She had spotted him the minute Corbin entered the sanctuary and bee-lined it over to find out if he was single. When she learned he was, she was elated and asked him to the single adults group. Corbin tried to be polite and tell her he was recently widowed and not interested yet. She was not easily deflected, but the service was about to start, so he excused himself and squeezed between his buddies and their wives so he would not have an empty seat next to him.

Sarah laughed, and teased her dad for being the new "hot single guy". They decided to call the woman "Lady Godiva".

When she told her dad what she was going through at school he told her,

"Sarah, you sound like you are overwhelmed."

"I am. I don't know how to get out of this hole I'm in. I need some help."

"What is your number one desire? Let's start with that."

"I want a friend."

"Okay, Let's ask God to bring you a friend that will love you for who you are. But, you have to be willing to take the friend he gives you, and love her with God's love. She may not look like what you would pick out, but let's let God pick her out."

"Okay. I'll take anyone right now."

They prayed, and Sarah went to sleep with new hope.

3

The next day Sarah was in line in the lunchroom and noticed a girl sitting alone at a table. Sarah thought by the way she kept her head down, that she felt dejected. Her hair was jet black along with her clothes, shoes, finger nails and thick eye liner. She had way too many piercings. Sarah recognized from the quickening in her heart that this was her new friend. Her dad was right...this girl did *not* look like the type Sarah would be friends with. What could they ever have in common?

Sarah got her tray, and went to the table of Gothic Girl and asked if she minded if she sat with her. Gothic Girl looked up, surprised to see Sarah was talking to her. She quickly reverted to her shell, and looking down at her plate mumbled, "Sure."

Sarah chose *not* to let the girl's lack of enthusiasm discourage her. She didn't know what Gothic Girl meant by "sure" but decided to take it as a "yes". She sat down across from her and started opening her milk carton and much to Sarah's surprise, Gothic Girl started the conversation.

"What's it like being pregnant?"

Her question was not like the rude guy's at church. Even though it was a little abrupt, she was sincere, and Sarah instantly liked this weird gothic girl.

"Well, right now I'm too sick to enjoy it too much, but it has its perks."

"Yeah?" She said, looking up. "Like what?"

"Well, I'm starting to get boobs for the first time." Sarah said much louder than she had planned.

Sarah hadn't noticed that Jonathan had made his way across the cafeteria to speak to her. He arrived at their table just as she made her perky statement. He was visibly taken aback and didn't quite know how to handle the situation. He had his speech planned, so he went with it. "Uh...hi! I wanted to see how your first few days of school were going?" he said, trying to act like he didn't hear what she had just said.

It was all Sarah could do not to crawl under the table, but instead, she did what she always did when she was embarrassed and not in control—she burst out laughing.

It took a second, but Gothic girl also started laughing... then poor Jonathan turned three shades of red and joined the laughter. It was one of those magical moments when three people, who barely know each other, connect. Somehow, Sarah managed to say, "Thanks, my day just got better."

"I think mine did too." Jonathan said with a grin as he turned to walk away.

Their laughter had attracted the attention of the students in the cafeteria, who were wondering what had just happened. Sarah looked at her new friend and said, still laughing, "By the way, my name's Sarah."

"I know, I'm Rachael." They continued laughing and talking about the great timing of her words. The lunch bell rang, much too soon, and they said their goodbyes. God had answered Sarah's prayer. She couldn't wait to get home and tell her dad how God had given her a friend. She only wished Rachael had classes with her.

After school, while Sarah was waiting for her dad to come and pick her up, she saw Rachael in the bus line. Sarah ran over and asked how her day had been.

Sarah's Story

"It sucked, as always. How 'bout yours?"

"It was okay. Do you want to do something together this weekend? I'm going to be fixing up my room and wondered if you would like to help me paint it?"

Rachael looked a little shocked. Sarah wondered if she had ever gotten an invitation to someone's house before. After a brief pause, Rachael answered. "I don't know if I can. I'll let you know tomorrow. Thanks."

Well, it wasn't the answer Sarah was hoping for, but it wasn't a "no" either, so there was hope.

"Okay then, I'll see ya tomorrow. By the way, do you have a cell phone?" Sarah knew she was probably going a little fast for Rachael, but Sarah was so eager to have a friend.

"No, I used to but, uh, not anymore." Rachael said as she dropped her eyes to the ground.

"Okay, that's cool. I'll see ya tomorrow."

"Okay, bye."

Rachael got on the bus and Sarah's dad pulled up in his luxury car. Rachael watched as they drove away.

4

All the way home Sarah was thinking about Rachael. Rachael was so restrained and closed in some ways, yet refreshingly open in others. Sarah's thoughts raced. *Everyone has a cell phone. Even the poorest seemed to own a phone. Is Rachael poor? Would she be uncomfortable coming to my house? Does she understand that I want to be her friend?* She prayed, *Lord, help me know how to reach out to Rachael and be a true friend. Help me to gain her confidence and show her Your love.*

That night, feeling like she was up against impossible odds, Sarah got out her Bible and turned to I Samuel 17-18 to read about David and Goliath, a story that had encouraged her many times in the past. This time, David and Goliath faded into the background while the introduction of David and Jonathan jumped off the page. David had just killed Goliath, and Saul and Jonathan wanted to know who David was. After their introduction, it says that, "the soul of Jonathan was knit to the soul of David, and Jonathan loved him as his own soul." Jonathan had never met David before, yet they loved each other immediately. That was exactly how Sarah felt about Rachael. It was so strange. As she drifted off to sleep, she wondered if Rachael felt the same way about her.

Sarah's Story

Sarah often dreamed and understood that God spoke through dreams. He had spoken to her that way on many occasions. That night, she dreamed that she and two other people, one boy and one girl, were dressed in black wet suits. They were on a covert mission and had to scale a wall to accomplish their goal. It was night and this wall was in the ocean. On the shore, people from all different backgrounds were sitting in the grandstands, cheering. Although Sarah didn't see her mom, she knew she was in the crowd.

Sarah was awakened and reached for her journal she kept beside her bed to write the dream down. She asked God to help her with the interpretation. *Who were these two people and what was their mission?* She figured the girl might be Rachael, her new God-given friend. But, who was the boy? And, what was the mission? *God, do you realize I'm pregnant? How am I going to scale a wall in my condition? I guess You have it all figured out and I'll be the last to know. God, please unveil all this to me because I am a little cloudy.* She *did* understand the people on the grandstands were the crowd of witnesses the Bible talks about in Hebrews 12:1, who watch and cheer us on. God reminded Sarah of the prayer she had prayed in youth the night before. She had asked for a sign that God was calling her to be a leader. This dream must be her confirmation; leadership the mission. Sarah knew that with the hosts of heaven cheering her on, she would be victorious. *Thank you, God for your confirmation. You are forever faithful. You know how weak I feel, but, You are my strength.*

Sarah went to school early to talk to Rachael. When she got out of the car, Rachael was already walking toward her.

"Hi! I was hoping I could see you before school," Rachael said as she approached Sarah. "I can't come to your house this weekend because my mom needs me to watch my younger brother while she works. My life is pretty complicated, and I don't have a lot of spare time. I hope you understand."

Sarah's Story

"Oh, I understand." Sarah said, even though she didn't. She was sad for Rachael and disappointed for herself.

"So, do you have a dad?"

"Somewhere, I guess. I've never met him, and I don't know if my mom even knows who he is."

One thing Sarah liked about Rachael was that she was painfully honest.

"I'm sorry...I can kind of relate. My mom left last month, so it's just me and my dad."

"You don't know where she is?" Rachael looked appalled.

"Oh," Sarah said, laughing. "I know where she is...she's in heaven. She was killed in a car wreck."

Now Rachael was the one who was sorry. The bell rang.

"I'll see ya at lunch."

"Yeah, enjoy your morning," Rachael said, rolling her eyes sarcastically.

Sarah laughed. "I will. You too!"

Sarah walked down the hall. She needed only to endure three classes before meeting up with Rachael again over lunch.

As she pulled books from her locker, Aiden, the awkward guy from youth group walked up.

"That girl, uh, what's-her-name, is not a good girl to hang out with, you know."

What??? What did he know about Rachael? In fact, what did anyone in this school know about her? Had anyone taken the time to get to know her?

"Her mom sells herself for drugs," Aiden continued.

Sarah was infuriated and couldn't come up with a response. She just stared at Aiden in shocked disbelief.

"Everybody knows it."

With that, Sarah found her voice and exploded, "So if everybody knows it, has anybody done anything to help them?"

Aiden was taken aback and just looked at Sarah.

25

Sarah couldn't stop. "Maybe instead of judging, you should be helping. And I don't think who I hang out with is any of your business. By the way...her name is Rachael. She just happens to be the nicest person in the school. You should get to know her."

Sarah didn't mean to sound so sharp, but she was angry about what he had said and felt compelled to defend Rachael. Normally, she didn't lose her temper, but that was before the rape.

Aiden mumbled something about how he just thought she ought to know, as he walked away.

So, that's why Rachael has to watch her little brother, and doesn't know who her father is, and doesn't have any spare time. Now what?

This is way over my head, God. I know you sent Rachael into my life, so show me what to do.

5

At lunch, Sarah put her tray down across from Rachael.
"Hey, Rachael. How is the sandwich?"
It was supposed to be grilled cheese, but it had more grease than cheese.
"Hey, it's food." Rachael responded.
Sarah wondered if Rachael had food at home. She decided to start bringing her lunch. She needed to feed her baby something better than this. Just the sight of this greasewich made her want to puke. She decided to eat the chips... another no-no... and the fruit.
"Rachael, I really want to be your friend. There is so much I want to ask you about yourself, and so much I need to tell you about me. I just don't think we can do that at the lunch table."
Rachael looked down at her plate, "I don't get why you would want to be my friend."
"Well, for one thing, you are the only person who has been friendly to me, and for some weird reason, I like you," Sarah said smiling.
Rachael smiled back then added. "We have nothing in common except the fact that we are both rejects of society. But, if you are friends with Jonathan, you won't be a reject for long. He just happens to be the most popular guy at school.

Sarah's Story

Every girl would die to be his girlfriend. If you keep hanging with me, you might lose the opportunity."

"Listen, Rachael, my mom taught me to never give up a girlfriend for a boyfriend, unless you know he is the one you are going to marry. It's never worth it, so I promise I'll never do that to you. Besides, I don't get why he would pursue me. I'm pregnant!!!"

"I don't know, but you are very pretty—sorry if that embarrasses you."

"No, it just surprises me. Thank you! I'm going to remember that when I get all big and fat."

They both laughed.

"Rachael, can I ask you something?"

"Sure."

"Why do you wear all black, because you don't seem 'gothic' to me?"

Without looking Sarah in the eyes, Rachael softly replied, "Because it's the color of my life."

"Well, not for long. God is going to bring color back into your life and you are going to live again. You just watch and see!" Sarah said with conviction.

A look of shock flashed across Rachael's face. Sarah saw her disbelief.

"Well, you must be seeing things. Do you need to get your eyes checked or something?"

Sarah laughed and wondered if anyone had ever affirmed Rachael's worth. She couldn't wait to see how God was going to unveil the 'real Rachael'.

Rachael continued more seriously, "I don't know about God. I gave up on His help a long time ago. I think He gave up on me, too. I *know* He gave up on my mom."

"God doesn't give up on anyone, and I can promise you, there *is* hope for you *and* your mom. When I get my car I'm going to come pick you up and take you to church."

"Well, I don't know about that," Rachael said, then, "Wait...You're getting a car?"

"Yeah, we just haven't had time to replace mine. My mom was driving my car when she had her wreck, and I can't ride in hers because it's too painful. My dad wants me to get one pronto, so he doesn't have to leave work everyday to come get me."

The bell rang.

"Not yet! Lunch is my favorite class, and it's over too soon," Sarah said with a smile.

"See ya," Rachael said as they walked to the trash can.

After school, Sarah was waiting with Rachael when Sarah's phone rang. It was her dad. She answered thinking something must be wrong.

"Hey Sarah, I'm okay, but I am waiting for roadside assistance. I had a blowout that somehow bent my axle. I ate lunch with Pastor Michael today so I called him to see if he could help me with picking you up. He offered his son, who will have his little sister with him. The pastor assured me that his son is the utmost gentleman. Are you comfortable with that? If not, the only option I can think of is a taxi, and *I* don't feel comfortable with that."

As Sarah was taking all this in, she heard her name being called and turned to see Jonathan, who had pulled up in his blue truck. He rolled down his window, "Sarah, get in. I'm your ride home."

"What???" Sarah felt her heart racing.

"My dad called and asked me to take you home because your dad is stuck on the side of the road."

Sarah could hear her dad saying, "I think you might have met him in youth the other night. His name is..." and they both said at the same time: "Jonathan."

"So, you remember this guy?" Corbin asked.

"Yes, sir, I remember him. It'll be fine. He just pulled up. I'll call you as soon as I get home." Sarah said, trying to be brave. *So he's the pastor's son. Just my luck!*

"Okay, honey. I'm so sorry about this," Corbin continued. He had never felt so helpless before. He prayed an earnest prayer of protection for his little girl.

Jonathan had waited patiently while Sarah got off her phone.

Sarah turned to Rachael with a look of apprehension, but all Rachael offered was a smile of amusement. "You go girl!"

"Shh! I'm just riding home with him." Sarah said stiffling a grin.

"I think I see some color coming into your life, too. See ya tomorrow," Rachael bantered back.

"Yeah, see ya," Sarah answered. *I sure hope so.* Sarah heard a voice in her heart that said that everything was going to be okay, but her past was coming back to haunt her.

Sarah turned and started walking toward Jonathan's car. She looked up to see Jonathan beaming like he had just won a race. Sarah was feeling like she just lost one.

As Sarah was getting into the front seat, wishing she was sitting in the back, Jonathan started talking. "Your dad had lunch with my dad today...Pastor Michael McCormick." He added his name for emphasis.

"You're the *pastor's* son?" Sarah spit out, not able to think of anything else.

"Yeah, have been all my life," he smiled, wondering if she had a problem with that by the way she said it.

Jonathan seemed much different from Jason, her last pastor's son. Surely her dad wouldn't have set her up for another disaster. Still, she hugged her door...as much as you can in a truck.

"This is my sister, Bethany." Jonathan said as he motioned to Bethany in the back seat.

Sarah's Story

Sarah turned to peek at the adorable girl. She looked to be around 10 years old. Bethany had this wild, curly hair with green eyes. She looked like Rebecca of Sunnybrooke Farm to Sarah. Bethany had a calming affect on Sarah. She was so glad she was there.

"Hi, I'm Sarah," Sarah said.

"Hi, Jonathan thinks you're cute."

"Thanks, little sis," Jonathan said sarcastically, not seeming to mind what she just said. Then he turned to Sarah smiling and asked, "Do you have a younger brother or sister?"

"No, I'm an only child."

"Oh, then you have no idea how embarrassing they can be."

Sarah was the one embarrassed, so she was getting the idea all right.

"Do you know where I live?" Sarah asked, trying to change the subject.

" Yes, but first, I've got to make a stop. Are you hungry?"

"What? Why?"

Sarah *was* famished, but right now, she just wanted to get home as fast as his blue truck could get her there.

"Because, every Monday, my mom takes me to Sonic to get a cherry limeade. Today, Jonathan gets to take me," Bethany said, beaming.

Jonathan looked at Sarah, "Thanks for that information, Sis. Since I don't have practice today, I was given the privilege of taking Bethany home and doing the Monday afterschool ritual. Huh, Beth?"

"That's right! And, don't leave out the part where Mom gave you money for both of us," Bethany said smugly.

"Oh, yeah. That's right," Jonathan said with a twinkle.

"So, are you hungry? Because, I am," Jonathan said, smiling his irresistible grin.

"Famished!" Sarah confessed, realizing there was no way out of this. "They say I'm eating for two, but we both skipped lunch," Sarah couldn't believe she said that she was pregnant in front of Bethany, much less Jonathan.

"Yea, school lunches are for the brave with iron stomachs. I bring my lunch."

Sarah was glad Jonathan made no pretense about knowing she was pregnant. She hated pretense. It must have gone over Bethany's head because she didn't say anything.

"How about you, Bethany? Did you bring your lunch today?" Sarah asked, trying to include her in their conversation.

"Yes, I bring a peanut butter and marshmallow sandwich with an apple and wheat crackers."

"Yum!" Sarah said, almost about to lose her appetite.

"Yeah, that's what I say. She and my mother love peanut butter with marshmallows. It makes me want to gag."

"I will have to agree with you. I'll definitely bring my lunch tomorrow...minus the marshmallows," she said, smiling back at Bethany.

Jonathan pulled into Sonic.

"What do you want?"

It was then that Sarah realized she had no money.

"I don't have any money. Can I borrow some from you?"

"I tell you what. This one's on me. You can get it next time."

Sarah was thinking there wasn't going to be a next time.

"Thanks. I'll have a grilled chicken wrap with three ketchups and a water."

"Okay," Jonathan said, amused at her order.

Jonathan pushed the button and soon ordered. They sat waiting for their food in a silence that was deafening.

Sarah looked back at Bethany to say something to her, to break the silence, but she was playing a video game on Jonathan's phone.

"So...does your dad pick you up everyday?" Jonathan asked.

Sarah's Story

Sarah was wondering why he would ask. She remembered her counselor told her she would be more paranoid than usual. So Sarah tried to not read anything into his question, though it was hard not to.

"Yeah, so far he has. I need to get a car. We just haven't had time to look."

Their food came, and as Jonathan swallowed the third bite of his hamburger, he turned to Sarah.

"I have a question for you," Jonathan asked very seriously.

Here it comes. He's going to ask me about my pregnancy right here in front of Bethany.

"What kind of car do you want?" He smiled.

Sarah was so unprepared for that question, she almost choked on her wrap.

"I don't know. I want something sort of small, not too sporty, but safe."

Sarah cringed. How uncool was that? She was practical and conservative to a fault. She wondered what he thought about her answer.

"Okay, do you want standard or automatic; used or new; 4-wheel drive?

"Uh, I don't know. I just want something that is easy to drive," Sarah said, thinking she sounded like she was driving on empty. She knew nothing about cars, only ones she liked and ones she didn't.

Jonathan didn't skip a beat. "Wanna go look? I love cars, and just happen to know a car that might meet your approval. We pass right by Ted Smithy's car lot on the way home."

Sarah had seen that car lot everyday, so she knew just where he was talking about.

"Yay! I wanna go!" Bethany exclaimed. She was loving getting to hang with her older brother.

Sarah felt confined, but at peace. She heard her voice say, "Sure, I guess so."

Sarah's Story

A text came in on Sarah's phone from her dad. He was checking in on her since he hadn't heard anything yet. She texted back that she was fine, then she decided to let him know that they were stopping off at Ted Smithy's Car Lot. Her dad texted back that he was on his way, and would meet them there.

6

Jonathan drove up to the car dealership and pointed to a silver, sporty SUV. Sarah loved it immediately. It was perfect. *How did he do that?*

Jonathan just happened to know the salesperson, because he went to their church. He introduced Sarah to Mr. Tom Walker and explained that her dad was on the way.

The salesman pointed out all its features then asked if she wanted to go for a test drive. Mr. Walker handed her the keys and slipped into the passenger seat while Jonathan and Bethany climbed into the back. After her test drive, Sarah was sold.

She stood back, amazed at how easy it was for Jonathan. He seemed to like everyone, and everyone seemed to like him. She was beginning to like him herself...as a friend.

Corbin showed up, and after a hundred questions about the car and its safety features, Corbin was satisfied that Sarah had found her car. Sarah was happier than she had been since her mom died. How could a car make such a difference? Maybe it was because she had someone to share the experience with.

Her mom had always taught her that your car symbolizes your ministry. Getting a new car is symbolic for getting a new ministry. *I'm definitely getting a new ministry. Right now that*

Sarah's Story

ministry looks like persevering through persecution to me. Jesus, I hope there is more to it than that.

As Corbin was working out the details with Mr. Walker, Sarah, Jonathan, and Bethany sat in the lobby in the cushy red chairs.

"I noticed you making friends with Rachael Osborne," Jonathan said.

Sarah paused for a minute to see if he was going to warn her not to hang out with Rachael, but when he didn't, she replied, "Yeah, underneath all that black is a really sweet and hurting girl. I don't think anyone has taken the time to get to know her. I really like her. She's different in a refreshing way."

"I'm glad. Rachael needs a friend like you."

"What do you mean by that?" Sarah asked, "I'm the one that's pregnant. I need her as much or more than she needs me," Sarah confessed.

Jonathan looked a little embarrassed at her boldness.

"I meant, that I think you are brave to reach out to Rachael. You'll be a good influence on her."

Sarah teared up. That was the first supportive words anyone had said to her since she had moved there.

"Thanks," was all she could get out.

"You're pregnant?" Bethany practically shouted. Somehow this word made it past the haze of video land into her ears. "You're too young to be pregnant! You have to be twenty-five before you can get pregnant." She paused to look at Sarah's stomach. "You don't *look* pregnant." All this spilled out in one big run-on sentence. Sarah and Jonathan looked at each other and laughed. Finally Sarah said, "you're right. I did things way too early, but I promise you, one day, I *will* look pregnant."

Jonathan just gazed at Sarah, in awe of her honesty and courage.

"Sorry I have to go." Sarah said a little sarcastically. "You'll have to explain this to your sister, yourself... Good luck!" Sarah said with raised eyebrows, smiling as she stood to meet her dad.

"Thanks." Jonathan answered with a sarcastic smile.

Corbin walked up and thanked Jonathan for helping Sarah find a car. They walked out together.

"Enjoy your new ride!" Jonathan said as he drove off.

"I will, thanks!" Sarah smiled back. She could already hear Bethany bombarding him with questions as they drove off. *Ah, to be a fly on the wall!* Sarah thought.

As Sarah drove home, it wasn't her new car she was thinking about; her mind was on Jonathan. He was definitely a decent guy. She wondered if he reached out to every new kid at church like he had reached out to her.

That night, Sarah took out her Bible and it opened to Psalms 37. Her counselor had encouraged her to start reading her Bible out loud so her baby could hear the Word of God, too. She knew his little mind couldn't understand, but his spirit could. In the Psalms, David was encouraging himself not to envy the wicked whose life is too short. In the end, they would have nothing to show for their lives. Instead God told David to delight in Him, and He would give David the things his heart desired.

Her car was a total blessing, but it was just chrome and steel. Her heart was longing for something deeper. She read on and found that if she would give God her future, then He would make her His witness and bring her justice.

Jesus, I want justice for what Jason did to me. I feel so ashamed and dark. How are you going to turn the light on in my life? Will I always feel this way? Was what happened to me my fault? Where were you that night? Were you punishing me?

Sarah thought about all this for a few minutes. She felt the Holy Spirit's presence and started to weep. *I'm sorry God, I know you love me and didn't do that to me. I just don't know how to get these memories out of my head. Please help me!*

Sarah continued to read and the next verse held the answer. "Be still before the Lord, and wait patiently for him to act. Don't worry or be angry because it leads only to evil." *Lord, help me to trust You. I surely don't want any more evil to come into my life. I know Your Word says that You won't ever leave me or forsake me. I'm going to try to do what these words say and wait for you. I give you all my anxious thoughts. Help me not to fight back out of anger.* She immediately thought of her curt words to Aiden. She should probably apologize to him for her response. After all, he was just trying to warn her.

Okay, tomorrow I'm going to talk to Aiden. In the meantime I am going to rest in God and not worry. She imagined herself climbing into Jesus' lap and feeling his arms around her. Peace settled over her anxious spirit and soothed her like a warm bath.

7

Now that Sarah had her own car, maybe she could hang out with Rachael more. The next day she showed Rachael her new ride. Instead of showing the excitement Sarah had expected, Rachael just sat quietly. She had this blank stare and didn't seem happy for Sarah. *Have I done something to make Rachael jealous? Did my excitement about my car turn to pride? How insensitive, Sarah. You finally have a friend and you blow it!* Sarah was beating herself up when Rachael spoke.

"It's a very cool car. I'm really happy for you," she finally said, looking at the dash. "I've never had a friend, much less one with a new car."

"Well, you have one now. Anyway, whenever you need to go somewhere, I can take you."

Rachael just looked at her, a little overwhelmed, and nodded. Sarah's counselor, Ms. Jane, had helped Sarah to realize that Rachael may have a difficult time accepting their friendship because of her own insecurities. Ms. Jane had also helped Sarah realize how much she needed Rachael. She wanted to let Rachael know this without scaring her away.

"Rachael, this new car means nothing to me, unless I have someone to share it with. I'm just glad I have you."

Rachael seemed deeply touched even though she couldn't verbalize it yet. She looked at the ground, clearly uncomfortable. She managed to say a weak, 'thanks'.

Sarah had her issues, but Rachael had hers, too. Sarah could see how God was using Rachael in her life and vice versa. They were both having to learn how to trust again. Sarah thought that Ms. Jane would be proud of her.

After first period, Sarah waited for Aiden to stop at his locker and said,

"Hey Aiden, I'm sorry for how I responded to you yesterday about Rachael. I guess I'm a little too defensive. You didn't deserve that. Would you forgive me?"

Aiden looked surprised and said, "That's okay. I probably had it coming. I don't know her like you do. I was just trying to look out for your reputation."

"My reputation is not something I'm worried about at this point," Sarah said, trying to be humorous. "But, I appreciate your,"–she couldn't come up with a word–"concern." Aiden gave a nervous laugh. He seemed to appreciate Sarah's joke.

"Thanks," Sarah said as she hurried to her next class. Sarah felt better as she sat down and contemplated what had just happened. *I think I have been as guilty as Aiden. I assumed he was simply another hypocrite, just like he assumed Rachael was a bad seed. Lord, help me not to judge people. After all, Aiden's my Christian brother and he needs mercy, just like I do.* Sarah recalled how uncomfortable Aiden seemed. *I guess he's not used to people coming up and asking his forgiveness.* Sarah's mom had taught her that when someone asks for forgiveness, the only correct response is, "I forgive you." The thought of requiring Aiden to say the words, "I forgive you," made Sarah want to laugh out loud. She realized doing so would make her look more foolish than she already felt.

P.E. had always been Sarah's favorite class, but not here, and not now. Her gym teacher, Ms. Horn, had been given the

Sarah's Story

information about her pregnancy, and her mission seemed to be to punish Sarah for all the young teens who got pregnant before they were married. Sarah couldn't figure out if Ms. Horn was trying to make her apologize in front of the whole class for getting pregnant, or just pay the penalty for all the teens who get pregnant. In either case, she stayed on Sarah's back about everything.

Sarah definitely believed Ms. Horn had a personal vendetta. Perhaps she had some skeletons in her closet. Maybe she had lost a baby, or been pregnant out of wedlock. Whatever it was, Sarah would probably never know.

"Just because you decided to go and get yourself pregnant doesn't mean I'm going to treat you any differently," Ms. Horn said, which was not true, because she definitely treated her differently. Ms. Horn's attitude toward Sarah was both condescending and demeaning. Everyone noticed, but no one seemed brave enough to acknowledge it, at least not where Ms. Horn could hear.

After a particularly grueling gym class, Jessica approached Sarah and asked, "You couldn't get your mom to take you out of gym? I'd have mine complain to the school if I was *knocked up*." Sarah wondered if Jessica's jab was unintentional or if she knew about Sarah's mom and was trying to dig her talons a little deeper. *Maybe, she is actually concerned... but then again, compassion does not seem to be one of Jessica's "spiritual gifts".*

"No, I know this might sound crazy, but I'm trying to be Jesus to Ms. Horn and respect her as my teacher."

"Oh, so now you think you're Jesus?" Jessica said with a smirk as she turned to walk away. Looking back, she added, "That *is* crazy."

So much for thinking Jessica cared. Sarah walked away, licking her wounds. It was one thing to suffer through Ms. Horn's workout, but another thing to endure Jessica's drills. *Lord, do you see me trying here? I don't know what it's going to take to get a kind word from this girl. She seems to purposely misunderstand everything I say.* Sarah remembered what the Bible says about our enemies—they aren't flesh and blood, but powers and principalities and wickedness in high places. Sarah couldn't think of a better description of Jessica. She seemed to be evil incarnate, acted like she was a princess of her own kingdom and certainly held her nose up in the air. She knew that wasn't what God meant but it did make Sarah smile at the thought. *Okay, so, Jessica isn't my enemy even though she acts like one....Oh, why does this have to be so difficult?* Sarah started laughing at her conversation with God. She realized she sounded like the children of Israel, always complaining. *Okay, God, please show me how to fight this spirit of intimidation.*

The next week, at lunch, Sarah asked Rachael, "How about today? Can I take you home?"

"Uuuuh, I don't know. I live really far away. I don't think you want to go there. My house is in a pretty rough section of town."

"Listen Rachael, I don't care what kind of house you live in, or what kind of neighborhood you come from...I just want to spend time with you."

"Okay then, I guess you can take me home today," Rachael said with a shrug, trying to hide her excitement.

"Good! Tomorrow's Wednesday," Sarah pressed. "Do you think your mom would let you go to youth group with me? We could take your little brother, too, and he could go to the class for his age. By the way...how old is he?"

Sarah had it all figured out.

"He's five." Rachael thought for a minute. "I don't know. Are you sure you want to take me? I'm not exactly the churchy-looking type."

Sarah's Story

"And.... I am seventeen and pregnant, need I say more? Besides, I need you there with me so I'll have someone to sit with. Please go, Please!"

"Okay...I'll see," Rachael answered reluctantly.

"I'm going to take that as a 'yes'."

Rachael gave a pained smile.

After school, Rachael met Sarah in the parking lot. Once they were well on their way, Sarah got up the nerve to ask Rachael about her mom.

"So, Rache, tell me your story. I know your dad is nonexistent, but what is your mother like? Does she work?" Sarah wanted to hear Rachael's side of the story.

Rachael turned somber and thought for a minute, then answered very robotically, without feeling.

"Well, my mom makes money having sex with men so she can support her drug habit. My brother and I are a huge mistake she wishes would have never happened. So...we are, more or less, on our own. My Granny tries to help when she can, but she lives alone and struggles to pay her own bills. She and my mom don't get along, most of the time. So, Granny stays away and comes when she knows my mom isn't going to be there. She doesn't know how to help my mom, and I don't either. I never know when I walk in the door if she's going to be in the bedroom with a strange man, or strung out on the couch...high. Take a left at the next light."

Sarah wasn't expecting this much information, but then Rachael was black and white—brutally honest.

"I'm so sorry. Can't they do some kind of intervention or something and get her into a rehab?"

"She's been picked up by the police before, and put in a sort-of rehab, but it never 'takes'."

"Of course not, she needs Jesus."

"My street is the next street, on the left. Sarah, I know you think Jesus is the answer to everything, but I'm not so sure even Jesus could help my mom."

"I know he can. I'm going to talk to my pastor about it, if it's okay with you."

"Sure, whatever! My mom's going to *love* that!" Rachael said very cynically.

"Rachael, are you ever scared?" Sarah asked, changing the subject.

"Duh...yeah. I've spent my life being scared! No matter how much I try to tell myself it wouldn't matter if I died; I'm still afraid of dying...I'm especially scared for Joey. He doesn't deserve to be in this family."

"And *you* do?"

"It's the third house on the right. Well,..." Rachael shrugged, "No, I guess not, but I'm older, and more used to it."

"Rachael, you don't deserve to be here either, and God is going to get you out. Do you want to come and live with me—you and Joey?"

"Thanks, but I could never do that to you and your dad. What would he say?"

"He would be glad to have you—*we* would be glad to have you."

"Let's just see how my mom is doing? As much as I hate how she is, she needs me—and she's the only mother I have."

Sarah suddenly missed her mom. She missed her every day, but when it came to things like this she really missed her. Her mom would know just what to do. Even though her mom was gone, Sarah was thankful for the kind of mother she had been.

She turned into a thin driveway that was more like a path overgrown with weeds. The grass, or weeds, hadn't been mowed in weeks; the shutters were deteriorating and barely hanging on; the screens on the windows were all ripped and

Sarah's Story

some of the windows were broken. It looked like it should have been condemned long ago. No wonder Rachael didn't want her to see this.

"So this is my haven...or should I say 'welcome to hell'." *Now what?* Did Sarah dare go in and risk never coming out? Did she insist Rachael pack her and Joey's bag and take them home with her? *Lord, what do I do? I could really use some help here.*

"Do you think your mom is here?" Sarah asked, stalling for time.

"I don't know; let me go in and see. I'll come back and tell you."

Whew, that was close. Thank you, Lord.

Rachael disappeared into the house and came back in a few minutes.

"She's not home. You can come in if you want."

In reality, Sarah didn't. She would have liked to be anywhere but here, but instead, she found herself saying, "Sure, I'd love to."

Rachael led Sarah into a very dark house. Sarah figured they hadn't paid their electricity bill, because no lights were on, and Rachael didn't bother to turn any on. It was the smallest house Sarah had ever seen. Everything was everywhere so it was hard to know where the couch was, or a chair, or even which room was which.

"Here's my room," Rachael announced, leading her into a very small bedroom. It was obvious that Rachael shared it with her brother. There were two mattresses on the floor, the beds were both unmade, and by the smell she knew that Joey had had a few accidents. Clothes were everywhere, because their closet was tiny and it was full of...stuff. There was a beat-up dresser on one wall with all kinds of makeup, empty glasses, hair brushes, and random clutter. *This must be where Rachael sits to apply her black eyeliner,* Sarah thought. Everywhere Sarah looked there was stuff, stuff, stuff! It made

45

her want to get out and go back to her organized life. Her life might be a little complicated right now, but at least it was somewhat orderly. This was a mess! What could she say about this?

"So, this is where you hang. It looks like you," Sarah said, trying to sound upbeat.

That was all Sarah could come up with. In truth, it did look like Rachael. The room was marked with expressive-looking artwork; some were drawn straight onto the walls, and others on lined paper or construction paper attached to the wall with straight pins or scotch tape. Sarah saw one disturbing painting that said, 'I hate my life'.

"Yeah, as soon as I can get a job and save up some money, I'm taking Joey and we are going to find a place of our own. I hate living here."

Sarah couldn't blame her.

"The invitation is always open. You can come live with me."

"Thanks, Sarah."

Sarah didn't know what else to do. This whole scene was so unsettling. She told Rachael she should be getting home and left.

When she got out to her car, she remembered she wanted to give Rachael something. She ran back to the front door and knocked. Rachael opened the door.

"I forgot, I bought this for you." Sarah said holding out a book to Rachael. "It's a Bible. I marked where you could start reading. I figured you might not have one. We can talk about what you read tomorrow if you want."

Rachael had tears in her eyes. She reached out and took it.

"Thank you," was all she could choke out.

Sarah smiled, "See ya tomorrow" and she ran back to her car. She was famished. She had meant to stop and get them both something to eat but their conversation made her forget her growling stomach.

8

It was beginning to get dark when Sarah's dad got home. Sarah didn't like being by herself at night. She had never been afraid to be home alone until the rape. Now she had new fears. Corbin did his best to be home early every day.

While eating supper, Sarah told her dad about her experience taking Rachael home.

Sarah could not imagine growing up in a family like Rachael's. The Levine's had been an exceptionally close family, because Corbin and Kathy included Sarah in their lives, and were always straight with her. They taught her to make good decisions and allowed her to make mistakes, even though it wasn't what they wanted for her. Sarah appreciated that and learned from her errors.

"Can Rachael and Joey come live with us?"

Her dad listened and thought about it. "I want to help your friend too, but I want to do it in a way that will help the whole family. Let's ask the pastor what they have set up to help people like Rachael and her family and what we can do."

"Okay, but we need to pray that Rachael's mom will let her come to church tomorrow night."

"We can do that."

They prayed together about all the things that were bothering them. Sarah and her dad had never been close like this before her mom died. She had always relied on her mom to pray with her about things, but that wasn't possible anymore.

The next day was extremely difficult. Sarah was running late to school because she was fixing lunch for her and Rachael, so she didn't get to see Rachael that morning. She had to run out of calculus twice to throw up, and got in trouble for falling asleep in the next two classes. *I'll be so glad when I get out of these first three months.* Jessica approached her in the hall and wanted to know if she was having a girl or a boy. When Sarah told her she didn't know, she wanted to know if there would be a shower. Jessica's mom had told her that she didn't think girls who had babies out of wedlock should have a baby shower. It promoted tolerance for what was wrong. *What did I think about it?*

Sarah would have loved to say what she thought about Jessica and her mother, but she knew it would not be edifying. Instead, she told Jessica, she and her mother didn't need to worry because she wasn't having a shower, which was true. Who would she invite anyway?

She had learned that her nemesis was Jessica Smith. Along with being the school gossip queen, Jessica was also head cheerleader, Student Council Vice-president, and a whole lot more. She wore her friends like a charm bracelet.

To make matters worse, Sarah overheard some of Jessica's groupies talking at the lockers. One of them said, "I wonder if that pregnant girl is still sleeping with her boyfriend." Another girl replied, "I heard that he went to college and that she goes up on the weekends and stays with him in his dorm."

How do they come up with this stuff? Sarah wondered. Even though it was preposterous, it still hurt. No one had ever asked her the truth, not even Rachael, which she found odd. She wanted to know everything about Rachael, but Rachael seemed content to know nothing about her...so she thought.

Sarah's Story

She beat Rachael to the lunchroom and grabbed Rachael by the arm before she could go through the line. "I brought us lunch, so let's go outside and eat." Rachael seemed delighted, and followed her. It was a beautiful sunny day, so they found a place in the grass, away from everyone. Sarah thought that this would be the day she told Rachael everything about her pregnancy, but God had other plans. When they sat down, Sarah noticed that Rachael had brought her Bible.

As Sarah was unpacking their turkey sandwiches, fruit and water, Rachael started in with her questions, "I don't understand this book. I started reading in Matthew where you marked, and there were a bunch of names that were the father of so-and-so and the father of so-and-so. It said that Jesus was the son of David, but that Joseph and Mary were his parents. I always thought that God was Jesus' father. I am so confused!" Sarah laughed.

"Let me see your Bible." Sarah read the parts she was talking about and it *was* confusing. She realized that Rachael had never read the Bible before, much less had it explained to her. Sarah would do her best to help her.

"Let's start with David. David was one of the first kings of Israel, and he loved God with all his heart. He was a shepherd and wrote hundreds of songs to God while he was out in the fields watching his sheep. Many of them are in Psalms."

Sarah stopped to show her how to find Psalms in the middle of the Bible. She continued.

"God promised David that, through his bloodline, the Messiah would come, and that is why Jesus is a son of David. It just means they have the same bloodline."

"Oh, okay. I get that part."

"Now, about Mary and Joseph." Sarah continued. "The Holy Spirit came upon Mary and she became pregnant, making Jesus the son of God."

"I have another question. I read that when the Holy Spirit made Mary pregnant, Joseph didn't want to marry her. Why did the Holy Spirit make Mary pregnant then just leave her with a man who didn't want to marry her? That didn't seem fair."

Wow! Rachael was bringing up questions most had never dared to ask, but she was right. It didn't seem fair. It made Sarah think of the unfairness of her own situation. Then she had another thought. *Mary wasn't alone. God was with her and even inside her just like the Holy Spirit is with me forming Christ inside of me. If God could use that unfair situation to bring the Messiah into the world, he can use my unfair situation to birth something great too.* She wanted so desperately to change the topic to herself, but knew this was not the time. This was a divine moment, and she needed to let the Holy Spirit have *His* way, not hers.

"That is a great question." Sarah turned to Luke and read about the angel who came to Mary, and told her she was favored among all women because she would be the mother of the Messiah. Sarah read Mary's response.

"See, It was both a burden and an honor to birth Jesus, and Mary knew it.

"I see; is that how you feel about your baby? Have you had an angel visit you and tell you its name? Does God still do that?"

Sarah didn't know how to answer those questions. Luckily the bell rang, so they had to gather their trash and get to class.

"I don't know, Rachael, but you've definitely given me some things to pray about. Thanks."

Rachael seemed pleased, then remembered, "Joey and I *do* want to go to church with you tonight. I didn't get a chance to ask my mom, but I don't think she'll even know we aren't there. What time will you pick us up?"

"Six. I'll take y'all to one of my favorite place to eat! My treat!"

Rachael smiled.

Sarah's Story

Sarah could hardly believe what was happening to Rachael. She was watching a person transform right before her very eyes and it seemed so easy. *I guess it is, when the Holy Spirit sets it up.* He had been working on Rachael a long time. Sarah was just the one with the watering can.

9

Rachael had left Sarah with numerous things to contemplate. Sarah couldn't wait to get home and think. She had been so busy trying to turn the other cheek with the people at school and recover from her trauma, that she hadn't considered what God had in mind for this baby. There were other women in the Bible who lived through humiliation and misunderstanding, but Mary was the one Sarah most identified with. Mary was an innocent girl who loved and honored God. Then she came up pregnant, and her reputation took a dive. Even Joseph, the man who had chosen her as his bride, was going to take back his offer. Mary found her strength in knowing that the Holy Spirit had planned this baby and it had a purpose.

Lord, I need to know that. Do you have a plan in all this, and does this baby have a purpose?

She immediately thought of Hannah. So she found the story in 1 Samuel 1 and read it. Unlike Sarah, Hannah and her loving husband, Elkanah, had *wanted* a baby. Like Sarah, Hannah was falsely accused. Hannah was accused of being drunk when she was really just crying out to the Lord. Sarah was being falsely accused of having sex, when really she had been raped.

Hannah gave her son to the Lord...literally. It hit Sarah that she needed to do the same. She needed to give this baby in her womb to the Lord.

God, please take this baby and use it for your glory. She continued to read. Samuel grew up in the temple, in the favor of God. He became one of Israel's greatest judges and prophets. The Bible said that whatever Samuel said, happened, or as it said, "came to pass". So Samuel heard from God correctly and spoke it, and God confirmed those words with mighty acts.

That is what I want this baby to do: speak your Word accurately and have You do mighty acts through him.

Then she heard God say, "Your baby will be a boy, and you will call his name Samuel. He will speak My Word to many people and turn their hearts back to Me. He will be instrumental in changing his generation."

For the first time, Sarah truly understood that she was carrying God's baby for God's purposes. Like Mary, the promise of God about this child would strengthen her and cause her to be confident and not be ashamed.

Sarah got on her knees and thanked God for this promise.

At 5:00, Rachael called. She was crying. "I'm sorry, I can't come to your church thing tonight. When I got home today, the cops were here waiting. They had put my mom in jail, and had called Granny. She just drove in from Ruston. Joey is crying, and Granny wants us to stay home. It's a big mess!"

"Is there anything I can do?" Sarah said, hurting for everyone.

"No—well, maybe you could say a prayer for us."

"Of course! Rachael, remember the Holy Spirit is always with you. He is your Comforter and He will be your guide. I love you."

Pause.

"I love you, too."

Click.

Sarah wondered if anyone had ever told Rachael that they loved her. She hoped so. *Holy Spirit, please watch over my friend and bring peace and order to Rachael's messed up life.*

It seemed like every time Sarah felt like she was seeing some kind of victory, the devil would come and try to steal it. She was *not* going to let him win this time. Maybe this was all part of the plan. One thing she did know...Rachael was being drawn to God, and God was reaching out to her.

Sarah remembered a promise she had read in Hannah's prayer: "The Lord sends poverty and wealth; He humbles and He exalts. He raises the poor from the dust and lifts the needy from the ash heap; He seats them with princes and has them inherit a throne of honor."

Lord, Rachael lives in an ash heap, will you give her a throne of honor.

Sarah left for youth with a heavy heart. Maybe Sarah would get a chance to talk to the youth pastor, Caleb, or better yet, Pastor McCormick, about Rachael.

She had planned to walk in just as the service was about to start so she wouldn't have to mingle with people who didn't want to mingle with her. Sarah had set a time in her head to go get Rachael, and forgot to change it. So instead of walking in when it was about to start, she walked in thirty minutes early. She had been so preoccupied with her thoughts that she hadn't noticed the lack of cars in the parking lot or the fact that there were no youth standing around outside. She flung open the door with more strength than she needed so it made a loud "thump" as the door hit the wall. Jonathan was there sitting up on the platform, playing his guitar and singing by himself. She couldn't help thinking he looked like a modern-day David singing to the Lord. It was dark except for stage lights, so Jonathan couldn't make out who she was. Sarah gasped in surprise.

"Hey!" Jonathan yelled, "Who is it?"

Ooops! Maybe I can just slip back out and not answer.
"Is that you, Jessica?"
Can it get any worse? Now he thinks I'm Jessica. He probably likes her. Boy, *is he going to be disappointed. He's probably going to think I planned this so I could be alone with him again.* Pause. *I have to say something!!!*
"No, it's me, Sarah. I guess I got mixed up on the times. I'll come back later." She quickly turned to leave.
"Wait! Wait! I want to talk to you."
Oh, no! Her chest tightened and she was having a hard time breathing. The walls were closing in and she needed more space.

He ran down the aisle and met her at the door. She had opened it, so they wouldn't be alone there in the dark.

Sarah looked at him, trying to appear calm, and waited. He was the one who said he wanted to talk to her, and now he acted like he didn't have anything to say. That's because he didn't. He just didn't want her to leave.

"I asked Rachael to come tonight, and she was going to, until her mom got arrested," Sarah said to break the silence and turn the attention away from them.

"She got arrested? For what?"

"I don't know. Prostitution? Drugs? I don't know," Sarah shrugged.

"How is Rachael doing?" Jonathan sounded really concerned.

"She's with her Granny—she and her brother. We need to pray for them and get them out of that situation. I was hoping to talk to a pastor about that."

"Let's go talk to my dad right now. He'll know what to do."

"That would be great! Thanks."

Jonathan walked her to the building with the offices, and down the hall to his dad's office making small talk along the way. It was handy having friends in high places.

He didn't even knock; He just went right in.

Sarah's Story

"Hey Dad, this is Sarah, the girl I told you about."

That could be a good thing or a bad thing.

Pastor Michael McCormick was in his big office chair, sitting behind his big desk. He looked like he had been studying, probably for tonight's sermon, because he had his big Bible open. He immediately got up and rounded the desk with his hand extended to Sarah.

"It is a pleasure to finally get to meet you. I've heard nice things about you."

And, probably some not-so-nice-things. Sarah thought.

"Have a seat. What can I do for you?"

Sarah and Jonathan sat in the wingback chairs that had been strategically placed right in front of Pastor McCormick's desk.

Jonathan looked at Sarah as if to say, "Take it away!"

Sarah took in a breath and started. "Well, I have this friend at school whose mother is single and she just got arrested...for drugs, probably. My friend has a brother who is five and they are staying with their Granny. They are all very poor and need help. Can the church do anything to help them?"

"Are we talking about the Osborne family?"

"Yes sir, we are." *He knows Rachael's family?*

"First, I want to say that I think it is wonderful that you are reaching out to them. I've known Crystal, Rachael's mother, since Jr. High. She came from a very rough background, and I'm afraid the church hasn't done much to reach out to her and her family. It's time we change that and start living the gospel."

Pastor Michael continued, "We *do* have a ministry to help those in need, and we have a program called 'Celebrate Recovery' which would be excellent for Rachael's mom. The thing is, she has to attend voluntarily. Incarceration may be an incentive for her to do something about her problem. I tell you what...I'll talk to Stan Thomas. He's in charge of the program. I'll see if he can go visit her, or send a woman to talk to her in jail. We'll do what we can and let God do the rest."

Sarah's Story

"Thank you, sir. That's all I can ask." Sarah was more than impressed with her new pastor and the way this church was equipped to help the helpless.

When they got outside of Pastor McCormick's office, Sarah wanted to jump up and down and kiss Jonathan—*whoa! Calm down, Sarah!*

Jonathan looked pleased, himself.

"Sarah, you just don't seem like the kind of girl who would give her virginity away."

She could tell by his face he hadn't thought that one out before he said it, and wished he hadn't.

Sarah was also caught off guard, but recovered. She knew she would have to tell her story, but she was planning to tell Rachael first, not a boy, much less the pastor's son.

"I didn't." Sarah said looking into his eyes.

It took Jonathan a moment to understand what she was saying.

"You mean someone forced this on you?"

All the shame and memory came rushing back into Sarah's mind. She dropped her eyes. The air got thin and neither knew what to say. Sarah dreaded the thought that Jonathan would not believe her. Would he think she could have avoided it... could she have avoided it? These questions haunted Sarah.

Sarah's counselor had told her that she had nothing to be ashamed of. She had been violated. She encouraged Sarah to talk about her experience to someone she trusted. Sarah never thought the first one she would share this with would be Jonathan.

Jonathan felt like the breath had been knocked out of him.

"Oh," was all he could say.

Then he tried to recover, "I'm so sorry. That shouldn't happen to anyone, especially someone like you."

Sarah blinked away the tears but she managed to respond. "You're right. That should never happen to anyone."

Why was he always saying the right thing? Sarah was trying to not like this pastor's son, but he was making it very difficult. *Maybe that is my next lesson: All pastor's sons are not alike.*

Jonathan could feel Sarah's discomfort. Much to her relief, he changed the subject. He had enough information to process, for now. They were almost back to the youth room. As Jonathan opened the door for Sarah, he asked, "Have you met any of the kids in the youth yet?"

"Only Aiden and Jessica, but I don't think I made a good impression on either of them."

"Aiden is a little awkward, but means well. Jessica is another story. She is probably jealous of you, honestly."

"No way anyone is jealous of me. Does she want to be pregnant or something?"

"No, she and I have history, and I'm sure she doesn't like me giving you my attention."

"Is that what you are doing?"

Now, why did I say that? Sarah was mortified. The last thing she wanted to do was to flirt with Jonathan. Couldn't they just be friends?

Jonathan turned a little red and said sheepishly, "I hope so." Then he grinned his irresistible grin.

Now it was Sarah's turn to blush, and change the subject. "So, who are you going to introduce me to?"

Jonathan jolted back to the present and took her around the room, introducing her to people she had seen at school, and a few she hadn't. Most of them acted like they had never seen her before, and hadn't spent hours talking about her... speculating how she got pregnant. She was having a hard time not thinking she was meeting the Sanhedrin who had already pronounced her "guilty".

10

Jonathan was right about one thing...Jessica hated her. She watched Sarah the whole night. She would whisper to her friends, then look her way. Fortunately, the service made up for the persecution she was getting. It was just what Sarah needed. The youth pastor, Caleb, talked about Samuel and how we needed a generation of men who were willing to "live" in the presence of God and speak truth to their generation like Samuel did. What a confirmation for Sarah! Jonathan was busy helping Pastor Caleb with the sound equipment, so Sarah slipped out when it was over and went to find her dad.

Sarah had wanted to call Rachael's granny when she got out of youth group, but it was after nine, and her dad told her it would be better not to call that late. She told her dad about her visit with the pastor. She tried to downplay Jonathan's role, but her dad saw through her efforts. He could tell she liked him. What was there not to like about Jonathan? He was just about perfect, even if he was a pastor's son. She would deal with that when she needed to—not now.

She and her dad prayed for Rachael and her family that night. She didn't tell her dad what the Lord had told her about her baby. They had never even discussed what would happen to the baby once he was born. One thing at a time. They had enough to process with the rape, the passing of her mom, the move, and the pregnancy. The good thing was, Lady Godiva, or Lady G, which was what they decided to shorten it to, had not attended that week. Corbin heard she was out of town, so he got a reprieve! This made them both laugh.

Sarah woke up to the sound of rain on her roof. It rained a lot in Louisiana. Rain or not, Sarah couldn't wait to talk to Rachael. Much to her disappointment, Rachael didn't come to school. *What a long day this is going to be. If only Rachael had a cell phone!* Lunch was going to be excruciatingly lonely, so Sarah devised a plan to go see the school counselor. She could come up with a problem—she had plenty. Only the counselor was not available, so she had to schedule it for another day. Sarah told them she would have to get back with them. She was doomed to spend lunchtime alone. She decided to go through the line and get some milk. That would take up about six minutes. Then she would take it outside, and find a place to sit on a bench by someone she didn't know. Hopefully, it would look like she wasn't sitting alone. What did she really care? Only, she *did* care, which was the problem. She cared more about people feeling sorry for her than she cared about eating alone. Then she remembered what she had read the other day about not fretting. She decided to trust God. *God, You are the only one that really matters.* All that planning and fretting wasn't necessary, because Jonathan was standing at the lunchroom door waiting for her. "I noticed that Rachael wasn't here, and I thought you might like someone to eat with. I brought my lunch, too, so we can just take it outside." By this time, the rain had stopped and the air was humid.

She could feel Jessica's stare as she and Jonathan walked together out of the cafeteria. "Thanks!" Sarah said, once they got outside. "I was dreading lunch."

"I figured."

They found a huge rock and settled on it with their lunches.

Sarah's Story

Sarah continued, "How is it that you know just what to do, and just what to say? Did you take a charm course in Jr. High, that I somehow missed?"

Jonathan laughed.

"I used to wonder the same thing about my dad, so I guess, I just watched him and learned."

"You learned well."

He smiled. "I take it, that's a compliment?"

"Yes, that's a compliment. I don't give those out too freely, so you better take it and run."

He laughed again.

"You know, you are not like any of the girls I have ever met."

"I know...I'm pregnant."

Jonathan chuckled. "And there's that. Does the guy who... uh...got you pregnant know you are pregnant?"

"No, it happened right before we moved here...the very *night* before. I haven't seen him, or talked to him since."

"So, you know this guy? He's not just some random guy off the street that attacked you? I'm sorry. Do you even want to talk about this? It's none of my business. I just keep thinking about you, I mean–'it'." Jonathan said, catching himself.

"No, actually, it's freeing to talk about it. I have wanted to tell Rachael but every time I try, something comes up."

"She doesn't know? I feel really privileged."

Sarah continued, "I went to church with the guy–The East Grove Baptist Church of Plano." Sarah paused. "He was the pastor's son."

That was another blow! Jonathan sat in silence, slowly putting the pieces together. Suddenly, Jonathan jumped up, fists clenched, while his face twisted in anger.

"Jason did this to you?" He shouted.

Sarah's Story

Sarah's blue eyes turned as big as saucers and the blood drained from her face. "You know Jason West?!!!" she said in shocked disbelief.

Jonathan answered, "Our families were friends. Our dads went to seminary together in Dallas. We used to go to the same summer camp until two years ago."

Sarah was reeling. She felt totally exposed, and wanted to rewind this whole conversation. She never dreamed he would know Jason or she wouldn't have given the name of the church. *I should have sat by myself today. How could this be happening?*

Jonathan's anger slowly turned to dismay. "He's always been a little wild, but I can't believe he would do *this*!"

Sarah was devastated! She jumped up in her own defense and almost screamed, "Well, believe it!" Her face was bright red and her blue eyes were on fire. "That's the problem, no one wants to believe it, which is why I don't talk about it. And now you're calling me a liar? Well, I'm not lying, and you can stand by your friend all you want...but this is his baby and I didn't agree to this. Goodbye Jonathan!"

With that she was up, running to the door of the school before Jonathan had a chance to respond. She swung it open and ran down the hall to the bathroom where she cried in the stall 'till the last bell rang, then she went late to her gym class.

God, help me! I know how Joseph felt when he was thrown under the bus by Potipher's wife and no one in her household would stand up for him. She just hoped that Jessica hadn't gotten the satisfaction of seeing her rampage. *Oh, what the heck... I don't care!!!* Except she did.

Sarah would rather have gone through the rest of the day unnoticed like usual, only that didn't happen. Since Jonathan had introduced her to some of the youth from church, everyone was being pseudo nice. She was too overwhelmed to discern who was fake and who was real, so she forced a smile. In her last period class she got a message from the school counselor that she wanted to meet with her the next day during study hall, fourth period. *Perfect timing. Why couldn't she have met with me today at lunch!*

When she got to her car, Sarah couldn't dial Granny's number fast enough. She was disappointed to hear the answering machine but left a message for Rachael to call her ASAP. She went home and instead of crying, she took out her Bible and found some encouragement in Psalms 69. She read aloud:

"Save me, O God, for the floodwaters are up to my neck. Deeper and deeper I sink into the mire; I can't find a foothold... I am exhausted from crying for help; my throat is parched. My eyes are swollen with weeping, waiting for my God to help me. Those who hate me without cause outnumber the hairs on my head. Many enemies try to destroy me with lies... For I endure insults for your sake; humiliation is written all over my face... I am the favorite topic of town gossip... But I keep praying to you, Lord, hoping this time you will show me favor.

David couldn't have described Sarah's feelings any better.

She continued, "May your salvation, O God, protect me. I will praise God's name in song and glorify him with thanksgiving."

Thank you, Lord. I do know that you love me and you love this child and if no one stands with me, I will stand on your Word. I'm going to do just what it said. I am going to sing to the Lord, even though I don't feel like it. So that's what she did. She sang whatever came to her heart.

11

As she was sitting in her window seat enjoying the presence of God, her phone rang! *Rachael!!!* She answered the phone with excitement, "Hello? Rachael?"

It was Jonathan. He began talking, a hundred miles an hour. He was determined to get in as many words as possible before Sarah could hang up

"Hello this is Jonathan, please don't hang up. I got your number from the card you filled out last night at youth. I'm so sorry about my reaction. I didn't mean that I didn't believe you because, I do. I think you're the bravest person I know. You've been violated, lost your mother, found out you were pregnant, moved to a new city and faced the humiliation of no one understanding. I surely didn't mean to add any more hurt to your list. I am truly sorry for hurting you and want to be your support." Realizing she hadn't hung up, he paused and added softly, "Sarah. I believe you. Would you please forgive me?"

Sarah was unarmed by Jonathan's sudden tenderness. All her pent up tears came bursting out with a sob. Eventually, she choked out a broken "I forgive you."

Jonathan patiently waited, offering an occasional "I'm sorry Sarah. I'm so sorry."

Once Sarah composed herself she began to talk through her sniffles. "Thank you, Jonathan. I was just so afraid. I thought your only concern was Jason. I know I was more upset about everything that's been going on in my life and instead it all came out toward you. I couldn't bear losing another person so I tried to push you away before you could push me away." She paused. "I do forgive you. I'm sorry I misunderstood what you meant." With a little chuckle, Sarah added, "I might be a little hormonal."

Jonathan laughed a relieved laugh. "Thanks. I felt awful. I guess I *don't* always say the right thing. Huh?"

"Ha! Maybe not. Just proves you're human." Sarah said, with a big sigh.

"Sarah, I can't imagine how hard this has been on you. Does Jason's dad know? He would be devastated. Jason has always been self-centered, I just didn't realize he had become so brazenly evil."

"Pastor West knows, and I think he was more embarrassed about the police being involved and worried about the reputation of his family and the church. He wasn't concerned about what it would do to me."

"You called the police? Good for you!"

"My parents called the police. They were devastated too... it was awful. We all cried. The whole process was extremely humiliating."

Sarah felt like she was going to puke. She breathed out a sigh and continued, "That night, my parents had to meet with the police and Jason's parents. Jason denied what he did, and his father said he had to stand behind his son. He was his father—surely we understood. Well, I don't! Jason's parents agreed to pay his bail only if he would go to Teen Challenge while he awaits his trial. That's where he is now and that is why I don't feel obligated to tell them there is a baby involved."

"So, that was all that they said? What happened next?"

Sarah's Story

"We left for Monroe the same day. Three weeks later, I found out I was pregnant. A week after that, my mom was killed in a wreck. She had been crying on the phone with my dad. Right after they hung up she pulled right in front of an eighteen-wheeler. I guess she couldn't see for her tears." Tears were streaming from Sarah's eyes again. Every time she talked about her mom's death, she felt the impact all over.

All of this came spewing out of Sarah like lava from a volcano. Once she started, she couldn't stop. She couldn't hold it inside any longer. She was hurt and angry.

Sarah had distanced herself from her best friends back in Dallas because she was unable to talk about what had happened to her and she couldn't act normal either. There was no way they wouldn't be able to discern something was wrong. Although she didn't have to, she chose to get a Louisiana cell number and didn't share her new number with her old friends. Being defiled had done something to her. She felt robbed, damaged, unworthy, unclean, guilty and a host of other things. Sarah felt ashamed. She had become isolated and introverted, which was not her normal personality.

Jonathan was sick to the core. He had fallen head over heels for Sarah. He thought of her day and night. He couldn't understand his feelings, just that he wanted to protect her and take care of her. He hadn't counted on the child's father being an ex-friend/ex-rival. Things were getting complicated fast.

Jason and Jonathan went to a camp for children of parents in the ministry in the summer. Every year at camp, Jason and Jonathan liked the same girl, and spent the whole week trying to win her like a trophy, but this was different. Jonathan really cared about this girl. He thought it was a cruel twist of fate that now the girl he cared for had been defiled by, of all people, Jason West.

Jason had never been strong in his faith. His father sent him to camp every year hoping he would come back changed, but he was lucky not to get kicked out. He and Jonathan were total opposites. Jonathan was the spiritual leader, and Jason the cynical jokester. The last year Jason was at camp, he fell for a really beautiful girl. This time Jonathan lost interest in her. He couldn't put his finger on it, but she didn't seem genuine. Jason dated the girl for a while after camp when she tried to break it off. Not willing to end it, Jason went to her house to convince her and she ended up in the hospital. The rumors were that this wasn't the first girl he had beat up. They should have pressed charges then, but he somehow got out of it. His sins have finally caught up with him. Jonathan couldn't help thinking that if someone would have had the courage and the proof to press charges then, this would have never happened to Sarah.

Jonathan offered encouragingly, "Sarah, many people would have lost their faith in God, but you've kept yours. How did you do that?"

"It did the opposite for me. God has been my strength and my only hope. This is going to sound crazy, but I know God is excited about this baby. I just understood that recently, but it has totally changed the way I think about everything."

Jonathan thought for a few minutes then said,

"Well, I guess if God can tell Hosea to go marry a harlot, this is not that different."

"It is certainly beyond my understanding, that's for sure," Sarah agreed.

Jonathan changed the subject, "Can I ask you something?"

"Sure." Sarah answered feeling increasingly more comfortable with Jonathan.

"How did it happen? Where were you?"

"Well, that night I had gotten a text from my pastor's phone asking me to come to his house and pray for a girl who needed help. I thought it was a little weird, and since Jason gave me the creeps, I asked my mom to go with me. I told her I didn't trust Jason, and didn't want to go alone. She had plans that night, and told me to try to set something up for the next night. When I texted back, I got no response. My mom had left, so even though I was nervous about it, I decided to go.

There *was* no pastor, and Jason opened the door. He was high on something and when I turned to leave, he reached out and pulled me into the house. He told me all this stuff about liking me for years and not wanting me to leave. He kept trying to kiss me, and I kept fighting him off, begging him to stop, but it only got worse. It was the worst night of my life...I try to forget it, but I still have nightmares."

"Sarah, I'm so sorry that happened to you. I can't imagine how terrifying it was. Do you still have the text you can use as evidence?"

"Yes, I still have that haunting text. I backed it up on my computer so I wouldn't lose it."

"That was smart. What did Pastor West say about that?"

"He tried to ignore it."

"Sarah, can I share this with my dad? I need some help processing it, and he has much more wisdom in things like this."

"Sure. I like your dad. He seems like a real compassionate pastor."

"He is," Jonathan agreed.

"Oh, someone is calling me...I think it's Rachael!"

"Take it. I'll talk to you later. Bye!"

"Thank you, Jonathan. Bye."

Sarah clicked over to Rachael.

"Hey, Rachael!!! Tell me everything. Where are you?"

"Hey, Sarah." Rachael didn't sound very good. Sarah could tell she was crying.

"What's wrong, you sound awful."

"I am. The DHS came and picked up me and Joey. They say we have to stay at Granny's—which is in Ruston." Sniff. "I have to go to Ruston High. I started today and I hate it!"

Sarah felt her world come crashing down.

"You can't leave me!" Sarah said desperately. "Tell them you want to live with me."

"I told them, but they said I'm not old enough to make that decision. My granny needs us to live with her so she can get the checks for keeping us."

That is so wrong! Sarah fought back tears and was trying hard to keep her voice from cracking. "I can't do this without you, Rache."

"I know, I can't either."

"When will you be back?"

"I don't know, my Granny is telling me I have to hang up. She has limited minutes."

"Wait...what is your address?"

Click. Sarah could tell Granny had taken the phone from Rachael's hand before she'd finished the question. This was unthinkable. Sarah bawled. Her heart was broken all over again. What was God doing? How would she go to school the next day and survive? Sarah was devastated! She fell on the floor and cried out to God.

12

Corbin walked in that night to the sound of his daughter's broken heart. Sarah was sitting at the bar in the kitchen sobbing so hard she couldn't talk. Corbin's face showed the fear he felt in his gut.

"What happened?" He said, trying not to sound panicky. He quickly walked over and put his arm on her shoulder, waiting for her to get composed enough to talk.

She finally choked out, "I'll...never...see...Rachael...again!"

Corbin was a little relieved but at a loss how to help. "I'm so sorry, Honey. What happened?" He hated seeing his little girl so heartbroken. At times like this he yearned for his soulmate, Kathy. She would be able to comfort Sarah. He reached out and brought Sarah to his chest and held her. He shed a few tears himself. He could feel her pain. He just held her till her sobs turned to a quiet sniff. Sarah calmed down enough to tell him the whole story.

"I know it seems like the end of the world, but you will get to see Rachael again. Ruston is not that far. It's only forty-five miles away. I know it's hard to have so much going against you, but I have to trust that God knew all this before you met Rachael."

"Right now, I'm having a hard time believing God even remembers me down here. I sure would like to know why he chose to do it this way," Sarah finally sniffed out.

"Me too," was all Corbin could say.

Sarah went to bed, too exhausted to read her Bible or even say more than "goodnight" to God.

The next morning, Sarah shuffled down the stairs in her slippers and P.J.'s hoping to persuade her dad to let her stay home. Her eyes were red and puffy, and she felt horrible. She wasn't ready to face the school day without Rachael.

Her dad had spent most of the night thinking about everything.

"Sarah, you loved Rachael and showed her the love of Jesus. She now has a Bible, and for some reason, God has put her in Ruston. Maybe God wants you to reach out beyond Rachael at school. Rachael was your comfort zone, and maybe God has more for you to do—more people he wants you to reach."

Sarah took a bite of toast and thought about what he said. Of course he was right. Sarah just didn't want to put forth the effort and start over.

"You know Dad, I walk down the hall looking straight ahead. I don't even talk to the girls in gym class...or any of my classes. You're right...but I'm going to need some extra-powerful grace to do that," Sarah said unenthusiastically.

"Sarah, God will give you grace. You just give him permission."

Sarah contemplated that. "Okay. Woo hoo! Let's see what God does today!" Sarah said a little sarcastically. They both laughed. Her dad kissed her on the top of her head.

"Now that's my girl. I'm proud of you and your mom would be too. You are just like her."

Sarah wanted to cry. Instead, she packed her lunch and headed for her new adventure.

Lord, help me to see through your eyes today. Show me who you want me to talk to and reach out to.

Sarah drove up to the school and got out. She noticed a group of girls standing by the steps.

"I like your car," the tall brunette said as Sarah started up the stairs.

"Thanks...I'm...very grateful to have it," Sarah stuttered. She was trying to make an effort to be friendly. She sounded a little lame and uncool—but that was her.

"I'd be thankful for *any* car," the girl chuckled.

Sarah smiled. *Come on, Sarah, be brave.*

"My name is Sarah, what are your names?"

They all introduced themselves. There was Kate, the one who started the conversation, Melissa, Emma, and Christy. They all seemed eager to meet her.

"So, where is your friend, Rachael?" Melissa asked. Sarah realized that her life was an open book.

"Uh...she is going to be living in Ruston...family stuff."

"I bet you're going to miss her," Christy said sincerely.

"Yeah, I sure am."

"Well, if you need a place to sit at lunch, you can sit with us," Kate offered.

"Thanks, I think I'll take you up on that."

The bell rang. Sarah went to calculus and thanked God every few minutes for her new friends. God reminded her of the scripture, "To have friends, you must show yourself friendly." That was definitely something she had not done before.

She ignored the stares she got from Jessica. Finally, when the class was working at their desks quietly, Jessica got up to walk to the trash can, which was right next to Sarah's desk.

"I saw you and Jonathan fighting. I hope you got things *patched up*," she said inquisitively.

"We did, thanks for asking," Sarah answered as politely as she could.

So she had seen her explode? *I guess she is going to stalk our every move. I hope she can't read lips!*

As Sarah weaved her way to the next class, she heard the Holy Spirit say, *"Let my joy be your strength."*

Her second hour was Biology and today they were getting their lab partners. She hoped the teacher was assigning them, because if it was left to choice she would probably be alone.

She said a quick prayer. *Lord, give me the partner you want me to have.*

She was given an African-American boy named Tyrone. She had never talked to him, but she noticed that he always wore a big smile.

"Hey, little momma, I'm Tyrone!" he said with a big smile on his face.

"Hi, I'm Sarah. You might not want to get too close to this pregnant girl. You know, I might be contagious!" Sarah batted back.

Tyrone loved it. "Don't worry. I got my shots!" He said laughing.

Sarah laughed back. "That's good!"

Tyrone held out his knuckle for her to hit. "You're okay, you know."

"Thanks, so are you." Sarah returned.

Thank you, Lord!

Tyrone proved to be a great comic relief after her first period with Jessica. He kept her laughing. He turned out to be the son of a Pentecostal preacher. *What is it about all these pastor's sons? Is God trying to get rid of my prejudices about pastors' sons?* She thought so. Tyrone was full of joy, and it was him that was contagious!

During study hall, an office helper came to get Sarah for her appointment with the school counselor. *What appointment? Oh, yeah, only I never set one.*

Sarah's Story

She was about to explain that she didn't have an appointment, but didn't think it would help so she quietly followed the office helper to the counselor's office like a lamb to the slaughter. What was she going to talk about? She didn't have to worry for long.

She walked into the counselor's very organized office. There were file cabinets, a desk, two chairs and some really out-of-date pictures on the wall. The counselor's diploma hung, slightly crooked, verifying that Evelyn Maroney knew what she was doing.

"So you're Sarah. I'm the school counselor, Ms. Maroney," she said, motioning for Sarah to take a chair.

Already, Sarah was thinking Ms. Maroney should be working in a morgue with dead people, not with living, breathing, hurting people.

"Yes, ma'am."

"Yes, well, I have been wanting to talk to you, so I'm glad you set up this appointment."

You're the only one who's glad, and it was a mistake! Sarah chuckled to herself.

"I hear that you are pregnant. Is that so?"

"Yes, ma'am."

"You are not the first girl we've had here to get pregnant, but you are the first one to stay in school. I commend you for continuing your education which will greatly improve your chances for success later in life. The principal and I have had many conversations about your decision, and we have some concerns." Then she peered at Sarah sternly like she wanted a response.

"Yes, ma'am." Sarah gave her one, not sure where she was going with this.

Ms. Maloney continued, "We are concerned about what kind of example you will be to the rest of the girls and how you plan to handle the attention. Your influence could be detrimental to the younger girls, especially...not to mention the young men. This is going to be a distraction to them also. But, we expect you to be a positive example. The choice is yours and I'm sure you will choose the right one."

Sarah had never thought about any of this—just how it was affecting her.

"Yes, ma'am."

"We want you to know that your teachers are watching how you handle yourself in your classrooms, and have promised to let us know if there seems to be any problems. So far, they say you are doing just fine. But...you're not showing yet! Do you understand?"

"Yes, ma'am."

"We're finished here. You may go back to your study hall. If you need to talk, feel free to set an appointment," she said, as she reached for the file of her next "victim".

"Yes, ma'am." Sarah left not knowing how to feel about that meeting. As she was going over it in her mind, she found it humerous and started laughing out loud. Then she remembered she was walking down the hall by herself. She stifled her giggle, and walked back to study hall. God had surely answered her prayer. She didn't have to worry about what to say. Just "yes ma'am" six times!

At lunch, she spotted Kate and the other girls already at a table. They seemed to be looking for her, too. *Wow, what a pleasant surprise.* She sat across from Christy.

They were talking about some guy they all thought was cute.

"So, are you 'talking to' Jonathan McCormick?" Melissa asked.

"No, we go to church together. We're just friends," Sarah said, not so convincingly.

"Oh, sure." Melissa said, not buying it. "Well, he's a hottie!"

Sarah hated to hear them use that word to describe Jonathan. He was so much more than just a "hottie". She wanted to share who Jonathan really was, only she knew it would reveal her true feelings about him so she smiled instead and changed the subject. She shared with them about her visit to the counselor's office.

They laughed.

"Ms. Maloney is full of baloney!" said Emma, laughing. "She has never been married and never had children, so she can't relate to us. No one *chooses* to go see her. I can't believe she said that to you."

"It's okay. Now I know where I stand with the faculty of the school. I'll try to be a 'good pregnant example' — whatever that is." They all laughed.

Sarah knew they were dying to ask her about her pregnancy, but she wasn't quite ready to confide. She needed to know these new friends a little better.

They seemed to understand and didn't ask. For that, she was grateful.

They talked about their basketball tryouts after school. Christy started to ask Sarah if she was trying out, then stopped mid-sentence.

Sarah told her it was okay; she would try out next year. This year she would *be* the basketball. They all laughed and Christy seemed relieved.

So, thanks to her new friends, lunch went really well. She saw Jonathan sitting with his friends. He smiled at her and gave her a thumbs up. She smiled back.

13

Once Sarah and her dad were settled in to their new city, Corbin had called the pastor to recommend a counselor for Sarah. Sarah was having nightmares and was scared to be alone. The terror of that night haunted her and Corbin knew he needed to get her some help.

Pastor Michael had recommended Dr. Jane Thompson, who was a licensed counselor. She went to his church and counseled many of its members. Ms. Jane had a strong foundation of faith which she used to bring comfort and encouragement. She used the Word of God as the basis of her counseling and was successful in setting many people free. Her mission statement was Isaiah 61. She understood that it was the Lord's desire to bind up the brokenhearted, bring good news to the afflicted, proclaim liberty to those that were in prison and give them beauty for ashes. She often gave scriptures for Sarah to use to fight her fears and to encourage her. She made it easy for Sarah to be totally honest with her. She was a godsend to Sarah.

Pastor Michael had started meeting with Corbin every week for breakfast. He proved to be a great counselor also. His friendship was a great comfort to Corbin. That morning the pastor brought good news about Rachael's mom. A woman from the church had visited her in prison, and was trying to build a relationship with her. Crystal, he learned, was booked on drug charges. The pastor was really sad that Sarah had lost her friend, and sent an encouraging word to her. Sarah missed Rachael terribly, but was excited about making new friends. Corbin was glad to see his daughter happy and hopeful.

Sarah got a text from Jonathan wanting to know if she was doing anything that weekend. She texted back that she was painting her room, Saturday. His response: "I love to paint. I'll be there at 10."

Sarah texted back: "Well, I guess you're invited! LOL!"

His response: "Is this a BYOB? :)"

"No, I'll supply the brushes. :)"

What about that? Sarah thought. This Jonathan was weaseling himself into Sarah's life and her heart.

Sarah didn't know how to process this new boy in her life. The scripture Ms. Jane had given her for the week was: "God has not given you a spirit of fear, but of power, love, and a sound mind." She told Sarah not to be afraid of making new friends, even if they were guys. God could use them to help her heal. Ms. Jane knew about Jonathan and knew he was a safe friend to have. Sarah remembered the scripture and made up her mind not to fear.

It was fall and the leaves were putting on their fall colors. Sarah loved to watch the metamorphosis from her window. She related this change in nature to what God was doing in her own life. He was sure bringing change! She just hoped it would be as beautiful as the colors of fall.

Saturday finally came, and Sarah was so glad for a chance to sleep in. She was relieved she had told Jonathan, or he had told her, ten and not nine! By the time he got there, Sarah had the floor covered with sheets, and the brushes, rollers, and paint all laid out. She had taken the switch plates off and was ready. That was Sarah—organized like her dad. She was also very creative, which she got from her mom. She had two different colors of paint because she wanted an accent wall with horizontal stripes. She wondered what Jonathan would think. Probably that it was a lot of trouble for nothing.

He arrived with an old holey T-shirt with the arms cut out and tattered jeans. He was strikingly handsome. Sarah tried not to notice or let her mind go there. She had on a paint-splattered white t-shirt and baggy pants to match. She loved to paint! She took him upstairs. It hadn't dawned on her that he would be in her *bedroom*! Another thing she would have to push aside. This was a job, and he was helping her.

He was very impressed with her readiness.

"We are doing what?" Painting stripes sideways? You watch too much HGTV!"

"Yes, and you don't have to help, if you're going to complain," she said playfully.

"Yes, ma'am, I'm at your service. If you want a helicopter painted on your wall, I'll be happy to do it!" Jonathan said.

Sarah couldn't help but giggle.

Sarah worked on taping for the stripes and Jonathan worked on painting the other walls. She had picked two shades of turquoise for her colors, and planned to accent with purple and orange.

"Is this part of your 'nesting' stage?"

"How do you know about 'nesting'?" Sarah asked inquisitively.

"I read up. I'm a pretty smart guy." He said, sure of himself.

"I know this, too," he continued. "Your baby is the size of a peanut right now."

"Wow, and how do you know about that? Oh, don't tell me: you read up on it."

"I have been reading up, too, and you know, I am fixing to get really big and fat. Are you still going to be my friend when I'm fat?" She said, kiddingly.

"I hope to be more than a friend," Jonathan said.

The air got really thin. Sarah didn't know what to say. She couldn't believe that he would like her–*really* like her.

"Sarah, I need to tell you something now, before I get too involved, and change my mind."

Now what? Sarah wondered as she turned to look at him.

"I made a vow to the Lord, that I wouldn't kiss anyone till I'm standing at the altar. I just thought you ought to know."

Sarah had heard of it, but didn't know anyone who had actually made the vow. She certainly didn't expect to hear that coming from him.

"So, you've never kissed a girl?" She could hardly believe that!

"No, I didn't mean I've never kissed a girl. I just learned the hard way that kissing is not a good practice to start, if you want to stay pure."

"I think that is a great idea. I've never kissed a guy before," Sarah said, thinking out loud. "I've always been pretty afraid of boys, truthfully."

It was Jonathan's turn to be surprised. "I can't believe you've never let someone kiss you before! You've *never* had a boyfriend? I'm sure plenty of guys *wanted* to be your boyfriend."

Sarah was embarrassed. "Well, I've never liked the same guy long enough for him to be my 'boyfriend'. I didn't see the point of it. It wasn't like I was going to marry him in the seventh grade!"

"Sarah, I've just never met anyone like you!"

"Yeah, you keep saying that. I'm beginning to think I'm an alien."

They both laughed.

"So, does one of the girls you kissed happen to be Jessica Smith?" Sarah asked, putting pieces together.

"Yeah," Jonathan answered, visibly sorry. "We were going together last year, and our relationship started getting weird. I realized she was not the girl I wanted to spend the rest of my life with. She used to be a strong Christian, but popularity and cheerleading changed her, and she lost God in the change. She still goes to church, but Jesus isn't her first love—she is."

Jonathan continued. "I was more like a hood ornament, just there to make her look good. I started pulling away, and when she realized it, she tried to use her body to keep us together. I was never going to let that happen. By the time we went to church camp, I realized Jessica and I weren't on the same page anymore, so I broke up with her at camp. She's been mad at me ever since, but in a very sly way. That was the same summer God called me into the ministry."

"Well, that would explain why she hates me and watches my every move."

"I'm sorry, just try not to let her get to you. One day she'll come back to the Lord, and she'll regret being so mean to you. She has a good heart underneath all that...Jessica."

"I believe you. I'll try to remember that."

They painted on in silence for a while.

Jonathan backed up until he was right behind Sarah, then he said, "When you get big and fat, you can sit in the back of my truck and keep it from rattling."

Sarah turned around so fast, and Jonathan was ready. He had put some paint on the end of his finger. Sarah was pretending to be mad, and before she could speak, he wiped the paint on her nose. "You're so cute when you're mad," Jonathan said teasingly.

Sarah took her paintbrush and before she could think, she wiped the whole brush across Jonathan's chest.

Jonathan said with a twinkle, "This means war!"

They splattered paint all over each other, trying to keep it out of each other's hair. There was so much screaming and laughing that Corbin came up to see if they were okay. When he reached Sarah's room, he saw two turquoise teenagers sitting in the middle of the drop cloths, crying with laughter. "I just had to come up and see what was going on. Looks like ya'll need a hose."

It took them a while to get cleaned up. Jonathan had a change of clothes in his truck, so they were back to themselves in about thirty minutes. It was a perfect time to stop. They had finished the room and the paint needed to dry.

"Do you have anything to do for the rest of the day?" Jonathan asked, knowing she probably didn't.

"No, why?"

"I want you to go with me somewhere. I have a surprise for you."

"Okay!" Sarah said excitedly. She loved surprises.

Jonathan had already okayed it with Sarah's father.

14

They got in Jonathan's truck and started out.
Jonathan knew how upset Sarah was about Rachael moving to Ruston. He had done some investigating and found Granny's' phone number and address. He had contacted them to ask if he could bring Sarah for a visit Saturday afternoon. Rachael was ecstatic! When Sarah saw the sign for the exit to Ruston, she commented sadly,

"Ruston is where Rachael lives. I just wish I knew where."

"I do!" Jonathan said excitedly. "That is the surprise. I'm taking you to her house."

"Oh, Jonathan! Really? I could kiss you! Only we don't do that!" she said teasingly. Sarah was getting more comfortable around Jonathan. He was so easy to be with and now that the pressure to take the relationship to the next level physically was gone, she felt more free to be herself. "How did you find out where she lives?"

"I have my ways," he said mysteriously.

"Oh, okay then, I won't ask. I don't care. I'm just excited to get to see Rachael! Thank you, Jonathan, this is the sweetest thing ever!"

"You're welcome. I thought it would make you happy. I'm not staying. I'll come pick you up in an hour. I want to go to the hardware store where a friend of mine works."

"Perfect! Thanks!"

Jonathan had pulled up to a slightly nicer house than Rachael had lived in. It had overgrown rose bushes, a white picket fence that needed repair, and a porch with a swing on it. Rachael had heard the door of the truck close, and ran out of the house, right into Sarah's arms. "Oh, Rachael, I'm so glad to see you."

"You, too." The first thing Sarah noticed was Rachael's red sweater. The smile in her heart radiated out to her face. Sarah also noticed that Rachael wasn't wearing black eyeliner. She was beautiful and Sarah told her so.

"You look beautiful. I love your red! Let's sit right here on this swing and visit. I have one hour, and I get the feeling it's going to go by fast."

They sat down giggling and hugged again.

"I'm not kidding...red's a great color on you."

Rachael blushed and added teasingly. "I'm trying out a few of God's other colors." They both laughed.

They sat on the swing and talked nonstop. Rachael told Sarah about her mom, her granny and her new school that was excruciatingly snobbish. Sarah encouraged her to just be herself; someone would see how beautiful she was on the inside and on the outside and want to be her friend. Rachael had continued reading her Bible. She loved the Psalms, and she had stumbled onto Proverbs which had given her some new insight into how to deal with the people around her. Sarah told Rachael everything: the rape, her new relationship with Jonathan, her new friends—Kate, Melissa, Emma, and Christy, to which Rachael didn't comment—and what was going on at school. They laughed about her counseling session and about a whole lot of other things. Rachael's granny and Joey came out to meet them. Her granny seemed like a sweet lady and glad to finally meet Sarah. The time flew by and soon Jonathan was pulling up.

"No, it can't have been one hour yet," Sarah moaned.

"Actually, it's been one hour and forty-three minutes. I promised your dad I'd have you home by five, so we need to hoof it if I'm going to keep my word...Hey, Rachael."

"Hi, Jonathan. Thanks for bringing Sarah."

"No problem."

Sarah hugged Rachael again, and told her she would pray God would send her a friend. She reminded her to do what the Bible says, "Be friendly". Rachael promised to try.

Sarah got into the truck so full of joy and gratitude she couldn't speak. She just marveled at what God was doing in Rachael's heart...and in hers.

"So, was that a good surprise?" Jonathan asked, knowing the answer by the look on Sarah's contented face.

"It was a wonderful surprise. I can't thank you enough."

"It was my pleasure."

They drove on for a while...Sarah basking in her visit and Jonathan deep in thought.

Sarah noticed that Jonathan seemed serious so she asked him:

"Anything wrong?"

"No, but there is something I want to say that might not go too well." He looked over at Sarah with a smile he hoped would ease the seriousness, and said, "I want to tell you while you are in a moving vehicle, so you won't get hormonal on me, and run away like you did at school."

Sarah looked uneasy.

"Promise you won't try to jump out?"

"You know what? Just stop and let me out now!"

They both laughed.

Sarah couldn't imagine what he wanted to talk about, but she was curious, so she promised.

"Okay, drop the bomb. I promise not to jump."

Jonathan took a deep breath and asked,

"What are you going to do once the baby gets here?"

"You mean, am I going to keep him or not?"

"Yeah, I guess that's what I mean."

"I don't know. It's a big decision and I don't have the answer yet. If I keep him, my whole life will change. I may have to quit school and get a job to support him. Of course, my dad has offered to do that, but is it really his obligation?"

"Have you considered telling Jason and having him pitch in and take responsibility? Raising a child is a huge task, both emotionally and financially. It seems unfair to carry it alone. But, then you would have to tell him about the baby, and I don't know if you want to do that. Jason is not a safe person."

Sarah sat, quietly thinking. She *had* thought about telling Jason, but she was still so angry with him. She had talked about this with her counselor, but hadn't reached a conclusion.

Slowly she said, "I have thought about it...I've prayed about it and scoured the Bible for some sort of answer but I haven't found one. Jason's not the issue. He won't even help himself; there is no way he could help me or a baby. But, for some reason, I still feel I need to tell him. Why does this have to be so complicated?" she cried, holding her head with her hands.

Sarah continued, "The real issue is the baby and what is best for him. I've always wanted a baby, but I would not be the best mother right now. He shouldn't have to pay for the sins of his father. He should have the benefits of both a mother, father and a stable loving home. I don't know if being fatherless would be worse than not having a mother. A kid needs both. I believe God has a special plan to bless my baby in spite of what the devil has done."

"Sarah, I know you would make a wonderful mother to any baby, but I also have many friends who are adopted and they have great lives. It *is* a big decision and you don't have to feel rushed."

"Things were so simple and easy before this happened, and now my whole life is a mess! And, it's all because of Jason! I need to forgive him...it's just not that easy."

Jonathan reached over and put his hand on her shoulder. "I understand Sarah, I want to hurt him myself. You are one of the strongest people I know. I'm so proud of you. Don't worry, God will show you what to do."

15

Back at school, Sarah's friends were taking some heat for her. She walked up on a conversation Emma and Christy were having with a group of girls that were in Sarah's gym class. They were asking about Sarah. It got uncomfortably quiet when Sarah walked up.

"Did I stumble into something I shouldn't have?"

One thing about Sarah: she would rather just meet opposition head on than to beat around the bush.

"No...uh...we were just talking," said the blonde girl with pink tennis shoes.

"If you have any questions about me, I'd be glad to answer them."

The girls scattered so quickly, one would have thought she yelled "bomb".

"What did they want to know?" Sarah asked Emma.

"Oh, uh, who the father is." Emma answered nervously.

"We don't know ourselves, so we have nothing to tell?"

Sarah realized she had excluded her friends to protect herself.

"I'm sorry I haven't told ya'll anything about myself and my pregnancy. Here's the story. I never loved the father and I'm not in relationship with him, so he's not in the picture. He is pretty messed up."

Sarah didn't want to tell them about the rape, or give his name because all it would only fuel the fires of gossip. But, more than that, she didn't want to expose herself to painful judgment. Chances are, they would never even see Jason, but the world was getting smaller and smaller with technology and Sarah didn't want to take any chances...and rape is so shameful.

"Oh, I had no idea. It's too bad it didn't work out between the two of you," Christy said sincerely.

"Was your dad livid when he found out you were pregnant? My dad would have killed me!" Emma said.

"Yes, he *was* pretty upset. But he's much better now." Sarah was saved by the bell. Surely that was enough to quench their thirst for a while.

Sarah found out through their conversations that all four of her friends went to church together. They never asked her to come to any of their activities, but then, she never asked them to any of hers. They were just "school friends" which was okay with Sarah.

Sarah was starting to show, which means that her nausea was gone, but the shame was unbearable at times. It was no longer considered rumor, because the obvious truth was growing bigger and bigger right there in front of her and everyone else.

She still hadn't told Jason. That night while Sarah and Corbin were washing dishes, Sarah brought up the subject again.

"I know I need to tell Jason. I'm not exactly sure why, maybe so he can know what his actions caused. Is that right? Am I thinking right? I need some help because it's confusing. I wish someone in the Bible had gone through something like this so I'd have some grid to go by." Sarah was rambling and she knew it, she just couldn't figure it all out.

"Well, I think there *is* a person in the Bible who has gone through this. Remember the story of David and Bathsheba?

Sarah's Story

When she found out she was pregnant with David's child, she didn't try to hide it from him, but sent a messenger saying he was the father. David's response was poor but, let's concentrate on Bathsheba. In telling him, she was pregnant, she put the ball in his court. I'm not telling you that I think you should tell Jason, but if God is pulling on your heart to do that then I'll support your decision, but, the only way I'm agreeing to this is that I know you are safe and will remain that way. Do you feel safe enough to do this?" Corbin paused to think about the ramifications of telling Jason and suddenly felt ill.

"I know this might not be what everyone should do in my situation, but I feel like I'm supposed to tell him. And, I do feel safe thanks to you, my counselor, my church, Jonathan and Rachael and the fact that I don't have contact with him." Sarah said

"Okay," Corbin conceded. "How are you planning to do that? Do you want to write him or are you considering calling him?"

" I certainly don't want to tell him face-to-face. I think calling him would be the best way." Sarah was starting to feel a little panicky.

"Do you want me to be with you when you call? You need someone with you."

Sarah thought about it for a few minutes. "I would love to have you with me, but I know I'll cry through the whole thing if you're there. I think I need someone there who is an impersonal third party."

"Like Pastor Caleb?" Corbin asked, a little unsure he was the right one.

"No, more like Pastor Michael." Sarah said, thinking it would be more comfortable being there with a father figure.

"That's a good plan. I bet I could set something up for Wednesday night before church. How long do you think you will need with the Pastor?"

Sarah's Story

"About five minutes! Four for him to advise me and one to make the phone call."

Corbin laughed. "Are you sure you don't want me there?"

"Yes, I'm sure. I'd never make it if you were there."

Corbin grew quiet and Sarah knew something was bugging him.

"Are you okay about this? You seem upset."

"I'm just thinking, I need to tell Jason's dad. I never wanted to have to talk to him again, but it looks like I'm going to have to. He needs to know, also. He doesn't even know about Kathy."

Corbin sat there in tormented silence.

"This is not going to be an easy conversation either."

"Do you want me to be with you?" Sarah said with a smile, trying to make her Dad a little lighter.

Corbin looked up at Sarah and relaxed a little and smiled.

"No, but thank you. I need to do this myself. But, if you change your mind about me being there with you, let me know."

"I will. I love you daddy."

"I love you too, Sarah. I'm so proud of you."

"Thanks," Sarah said with tears.

That night was a rough one for both of them.

Corbin decided to tell Jason's dad first. Not only was that the order it needed to happen in, but he needed to get the phone number of the Teen Challenge Jason was in.

Corbin had prayed and prayed about this phone call. He knew it could go really bad or maybe just bad. He called Pastor West, at the church that Tuesday afternoon. Surprisingly, he answered the phone.

"Hello, Delton? This is Corbin...Levine." Corbin said as friendly and courageous as he could muster.

"Oh, Corbin, hello, how have you been?" Corbin could tell he was trying very hard to be cordial.

Sarah's Story

"Delton, I don't know how to tell you this, so I'm just going to come out with it. Sarah's pregnant with Jason's baby." Well, that was one way to get it out. Silence.

Corbin could hear Delton clearing his throat. "Are you sure?"

"Yes, I am. I wanted to tell you because Sarah wants to call Jason and tell him, if you are okay with it, and will give me the number to reach him."

"Corbin, I know I didn't exactly handle things well when this happened and I have wanted to call you and talk to you, but honestly, I haven't had the guts."

"You were right about Jason," Delton continued. "He had gotten out of control and we just didn't know what to do with him. I guess I had been in denial about how out of control he had gotten. Sending him to Teen Challenge was the best thing that could have ever happened to him. Anyway, if it's any consolation he seems to be doing really well now. I have that to thank you for." Pastor Delton stopped to catch his breath and wipe a tear away.

"Now, about the baby. I don't know what to say...uh, how is Sarah doing?"

"Sarah's doing amazingly well. She has certainly had her obstacles this year, but I'm so proud of how she has handled them. She has taught me a lot! I don't know what to say about the baby, either. I guess we're just walking this thing out day by day," Corbin finished.

"I just recently heard about Kathy. I'm so sorry. She was such a wonderful woman. I can't imagine you and Sarah's grief. Let me know if there is anything I can do for you and Sarah. Keep me informed about the baby. And of course, you can have Jason's number. He can have calls after six."

"Thank you."

He gave Corbin the number.

"Let me know what I can do." Delton added as they said their goodbyes. When Corbin hung up, he blew out a sigh.

16

That Wednesday, Sarah went to the appointment that her dad had set with the pastor. She walked slowly to his office trying to remind herself she was doing the right thing. She wished Jonathan was here with her.

Pastor Michael was his same fatherly self. He had a way of making her feel at ease with "hello".

"Sarah, your dad said you wanted to speak with me? I'm always glad to meet with you." He said it like he had known Sarah all her life and genuinely meant it.

"You know about how Jason is the father of this baby..."

"Yes, Jonathan told me."

"Well, he doesn't know that I'm pregnant and I need to tell him, only, I don't know how."

"I see. How can I help you with that?"

"I would like to call him."

"That's a very brave thing to do. Do you want to call him right now, with me here, or do you want to do it by yourself?"

"I want to do it with you in the room, listening to the whole conversation."

"Okay, come over here and I'll listen in, but first let me pray with you about it."

"That would be great!" Sarah said, relieved.

Pastor Michael prayed the sweetest, most simple prayer. He prayed that Sarah would have courage and peace, and that her words would be tempered with grace. He asked that Jason's heart be changed and that God would use this for His glory.

Sarah came over and stood as close as she could to Pastor Michael so he could hear. She didn't want to call him on speakerphone because that sounds funky.

She had his number on a sheet of paper, but was shaking too much to dial the phone. Pastor Michael punched in the numbers and asked to speak to Jason. He explained that he was a pastor and a friend of Jason's family so they went to get him. When Jason answered the phone the pastor said,

"Hello, Jason, this is Pastor McCormick. How are you?" Pastor Michael said politely.

"Uh, fine." Jason answered a little confused.

"I know you are wondering why I called, but I have someone here who wants to speak with you."

He handed the phone to Sarah and gave her an encouraging gesture to be strong.

"Jason, this is Sarah."

Pause. "Uh, yeah, uh, how are you?" Jason asked feeling very uncomfortable.

What a crazy question! Thought Sarah.

"I just wanted to call you and let you know that I'm pregnant, and it's yours. I thought you should know." Click! Sarah hung up. She was crying and couldn't hold on anymore.

She looked at Pastor Michael with tears. "I'm sorry. That was as good as I could do. Was it okay?"

"It was great, Sarah. Let's just wait and let God do the rest." He patted her on the back. "You did great."

It didn't go as smoothly as Sarah had hoped, but she felt relieved it was over. When she walked out of the office Jonathan was walking up to give something to his dad for that night's sermon. He was elated to see Sarah there.

Before Jonathan could ask her what she was doing, she offered, "I called Jason and told him."

Jonathan looked at his dad for some feed back.

"She did great."

Jonathan handed his dad the package and put his arm around Sarah and told her he was proud of her. "I know that was hard."

"I didn't realize *how* hard it was going to be. But, it's done and I feel better. I wonder what Jason is thinking?"

"Yeah, I wonder."

They walked in silence to the youth room, both in deep thought.

They were early, so Jonathan challenged Sarah in a game of Ping-Pong. He knew she needed to do something physical to help her cope with what she had just done. It was the best idea he could come up with. Sarah saw it as an escape from insanity.

"I have to warn you...I'm pretty good at this game and I don't mind beating you and crushing your male ego."

"You're on! And I need to warn you that I don't feel the need to be a gentleman when playing pregnant women."

"Deal. And, I'm sure you have played many pregnant women in your life." Sarah said stifling a smile.

Sarah started with an impressive serve to warm up.

"I see I have a challenge," Jonathan said with raised eyebrows.

"I told you. I could beat all the boys at my last church. I think you're going down,"

"I wouldn't speak so confidently. Pride goes before a fall."

"The question is, whose pride?"

They drew a crowd and Sarah won two out of three games, but they were all close.

"I guess we know whose pride fell." Sarah said, laughingly.

"I'm impressed. The lady can play Ping Pong."

"At least for another couple of weeks." Sarah bantered back.

In Youth Group that night, Pastor Caleb talked about the prodigal son. Sarah saw this story in a brand new light. Jason was the prodigal son who grew up in the church and decided to go his own way. He was at the "eating pig slop" stage in her mind. She was still struggling with forgiving him. She thought about telling him that she forgave him when she called, but then that would have been a lie. He didn't deserve her forgiveness...did he?

Jonathan was hurting for Sarah and Jason. He and Jason went back many years. He wondered whether he should call him and try to talk to him, or if Sarah would mind. He didn't know how to ask Sarah. She might go ballistic on him. She had only done that once, but he still remembered her wrath. She was pregnant and he had read that pregnant people weren't always emotionally stable. He would continue to pray about it.

Sarah was struggling with something else. She couldn't get Jessica off her mind...or her heart. She knew she should naturally hate her, but she couldn't. Jessica hadn't started being kind to her in any way; in fact, she was meaner than ever. She seemed miserable! Sarah had heard that she was dating a senior named Trey Cobb. Trey was a wild football player who drank and smoked pot. It was rumored that they were having sex. She hated to believe everything she heard, but Jessica had changed for the worse. She still came to church, but she dressed more provocatively and seemed "dark" and lost. How could Sarah help her? Jessica hated her. *I guess that is something you can do, God. I just want You to know that I am available if You want to use me.*

17

Forgiveness is sometimes a process that happens in layers. That's how it was for Sarah. While she was slowly progressing with forgiving Jessica, she was struggling with Jason. One night she was replaying the night she got pregnant in her mind, wondering how she could have kept it from happening. Was she responsible? She decided to call Rachael.

"No! You weren't responsible for anything that happened! Don't let Satan tell you those lies. Jason is the only one who was responsible that night," Rachael declared.

"I know you're right...do you ever wish you could go back and change the past?" Sarah asked.

"Yeah," Rachael said, thoughtfully, "I wouldn't know where to start, but then I think, I might not have met you or God, or gotten to see how He moves in families that seem hopeless. Then I realize, that maybe, I *don't* want to change so much of my life."

"I know what you mean. This has been a banner year for me, losing my mom and getting pregnant. But, if I hadn't gotten pregnant, then I might have been tempted to do anything just to fit in. Now there's no *way* I fit in!" They both laughed.

Sarah continued, "I'm struggling to forgive Jason. I wish he had been some stranger, not someone I grew up with. We have nine years of history together. We used to cut up in Sunday School and choir and go to our church camp together. I know this guy really well. He just never seemed to understand what having a relationship with Jesus was all about. He was too busy embarrassing his parents." Sarah paused. "I hate how I feel, now. I hate him."

"I understand, Sarah. Anyone would. He really hurt you. I wonder what made him do that?"

"I don't know. I do know that he was adopted when he was 4 and he was taken from his natural parents by the state."

"Well, I definitely understand that." Rachael chimed in.

"Rachael, I know I need to forgive him; I just don't know how. I can say it over and over, but it doesn't change how I feel. I know Jesus forgives him. Why can't I? Is it because I'm pregnant? Maybe that is a side-effect of pregnancy—unforgiveness!" Sarah was trying to be comical, but she was crying instead. "Do you have any suggestions? My mom always told me that holding unforgiveness is like drinking poison and waiting for the other person to die. It kills you instead. This is definitely killing me. I hate these feelings I have."

"Oooh, wait! I have an idea." Rachael said excitedly, running to get something. When she came back she had her Bible and was looking in the back at the concordance for verses on forgiveness.

"The Bible you gave me has this cool thing in the back." Rachael said almost giddy. "It has topics with the verses that deal with the different subjects. It even gives you the page it's on in case you can't find it—which would be me."

Sarah loved Rachael's innocence. Everything about being a Christian was new to her. Sarah already knew about the Concordance, but would never ruin Rachael's great discovery.

"So what are some good verses for me?" Sarah said with strained enthusiasm.

Sarah's Story

"Uh...let me find one in the New Testament. I understand them better. Here's one in Matthew 6:14 and 15, page eight."

Sarah could hear Rachael turning the pages.

"It says: 'If you forgive men their trespasses, your heavenly Father will also forgive you; But if you don't forgive men their trespasses, then God won't forgive yours." Rachael cleared her throat. "Maybe I should have found one in the Old Testament. What is a trespass? All I know about trespasses are those signs that say 'No Trespassing'." Then it hit Rachael. "Wow, Sarah, this says you *have* to forgive Jason!"

Sarah chuckled through her tears. She knew too well that scripture, but hearing Rachael read it and hearing her reaction made it more powerful. Sarah saw it for the first time. Jason had trespassed his boundaries with her and the Bible gave her no excuse not to forgive him. The Bible was plain and simple. Rachael was right — she had to forgive Jason, for her own good.

"You're right. I do. Would you pray for me, that God will help me do that?"

"Yes, I will." Rachael closed her eyes and started praying.

"God, you know my best friend, Sarah, is having trouble forgiving Jason. Would you please help her to forgive? I don't want her to not be forgiven, so please help her. Amen."

"Thanks, Rachael. That was the perfect prayer!"

"Hey, I just thought about something. Maybe it would help if you wrote Jason a letter, telling him that you forgive him."

Sarah cringed. "I'll have to think about that. It's a great suggestion...my counselor said the same thing. She even told me I didn't have to send it. I'll think about it."

They continued talking about other things for a while and finally said goodbye.

Sarah sat on her bed thinking about what Rachael had suggested. She finally decided that it couldn't hurt and took out a piece of paper and started writing.

> Jason,
>
> Even though, I hate you and what you did to me, I forgive you.

This does hurt.... Sarah looked at her letter and was not happy with herself. She remembered what the scripture said about forgiveness.

Okay, God, I know, this is not what forgiveness looks like. I can do better than this.

She wadded her letter up and threw it in the trash can and took out another piece of paper and wrote: *Jason,*

She stopped. *Now what? Do I just say, I forgive you, and that's that? It can't be that easy.* She sat looking at her blank paper with Jason's name on it and couldn't write any more. She didn't even like looking at his name. She finally looked up at the clock. It was after 10 and she was really tired. She wadded up her paper, threw it in the trash and told herself she would try again...another day.

The next day, Sarah was plagued with the letter she knew she needed to write, even if she never sent it. Somehow writing it down seemed more official and final. That night she went downstairs to talk to her dad about it. She walked into the den where he was watching ESPN. Sarah hated to interrupt him, but she was desperate to get this resolved. She found it hard to feel close to God, or to pray, now that she realized how much bitterness she had.

Corbin sensed she needed to talk, and pushed the mute button. "Hey, hon, what's on your mind?"

"I was wondering how you forgive someone who hurts you like Jason hurt me?"

Corbin pushed the power button. This conversation was more important than football. The Cowboys could play without him. "Now that's a good question. I've been wrestling with that one myself. I'm afraid I don't have a good answer for you."

"You want to know something funny? I asked Rachael last night for some advice—I know, that's a switch—anyway, she read to me the part in the Lord's Prayer where it says that if we don't forgive others, then God can't forgive us. I've read that 1,000 times, and I guess I just never took the time to think about it, but last night it hit me like a ton of bricks. I...we *have* to forgive."

"I know you're right. I think I have tried so hard to focus on helping you through this and getting over losing your mom that I've ignored that part. I've been thinking about it lately myself."

"I know we don't deserve Jesus' forgiveness any more than Jason deserves our forgiveness." Corbin paused, then added, "I have more than Jason to forgive. I have his father also. He was my pastor and my friend."

Sarah walked over and climbed into the recliner with her dad. She sometimes forgot the pain he was going through. She just wanted to be near him. She was crying, trying hard to be strong for her dad, but it wasn't working. Finally she asked, "Daddy, how will we know when we've forgiven?"

"I think we'll know when it doesn't feel like a knife in our stomach to think about them."

Corbin was tearing up now. He had tried to be strong for Sarah, but he was getting weary and very lonely.

"I know that God's grace is enough to help us through this. I just wish it didn't hurt so much."

"I agree."

They sat together in silence for a while then Sarah kissed her dad and went upstairs.

Rather than try to write another letter, she decided to ask God to heal her heart and her dad's. She knew He would tell her when to write her letter.

18

At school Sarah tried to be happy, and keep her struggles to herself, but somehow Tyrone always seemed to see through her mask.

"What's with the furrowed brow today?" Tyrone said as she took her seat in Biology.

"Furry what?" Sarah asked teasingly.

"Furrowed brow. You know, this," and he squinched up his face like he was real worried.

Sarah laughed. "You say the strangest things. Where did you get that word? From some Harlequin Romance book or something?"

"Harry what?" Tyrone responded, trying to act dumb.

The thing was, Tyrone was extremely knowledgeable, especially when it came to life.

Sarah laughed.

"No, my gramma always said that when we looked like our world was coming to an end. For me that might have meant that we were having beans for supper with no wienies."

Sarah choked down a laugh and tried to act serious. "I should have known it was a 'gramma' word."

"So, what's eating you?" Tyrone wasn't letting Sarah off the hook.

"I'm trying to forgive the father of my baby."

"Oh, that's even worse than forgiving Jessica, huh?"

"Yeah, and so far I'm not doing so well."

"My gramma always said..." He looked at Sarah and they both laughed.

"Now, don't laugh, my gramma was one wise lady."

"No doubt, look at her wise grandson."

Tyrone smiled.

"You know that's right! Anyway, she always said that when you forgive, you in no way change the past, but you do change the future."

"Hmmm, I'll have to meditate on that one."

19

Sarah had always worked with the five-year-olds in church. She read in the bulletin that help was needed with that age group, so she filled out the card and put it in the offering plate when it came around. She had also told the youth pastor, Caleb, that she would love to lead a girl's small group in the Jr. High department. Caleb and his wife loved Sarah and had gotten to know her heart. With Sarah's permission, Pastor Michael had let Caleb in on a little of her story. Pastor Caleb had no problem with Sarah working with the girls, but then there were the "church people"—those Pharisees, that only saw a pregnant girl wanting to influence their daughters toward evil. When parents found out she wanted to help with their daughters they complained to both pastors. After much deliberation, they had to call Sarah in and tell her she couldn't work with either group. They did it in a very kind way and Sarah understood their position, but it still felt wrong and she felt rejected by the church members. They told her she *could* work with the elderly. *I guess I won't be able to influence any of them to get pregnant.*

So is this what you want me to be available for? The elderly? Sarah complained to God.

She decided that if she was going to learn to be patient and accept his will for her life, she would have to be happy about working with the elderly. This was the only door God seemed to be opening, so Sarah walked into the Green Acre's nursing home where her church held a church service every Sunday. It was held during Sunday School time, before their church service. The room was full of wheel chairs and about twenty-five really old people. She smiled and many smiled back with toothless grins. An elderly man from the church was at the piano playing hymns. Many of the congregation had hymnals...a few turned upside-down. It didn't matter because they couldn't see the words anyway. They were howling out "Amazing Grace." Sarah started singing with them. They were so offbeat and awful, that it was beautiful. They didn't care what they sounded like or if they sang on key, on beat, or the right words. They were free and refreshing. Sarah immediately loved them.

A man from her church, who was a few years from being a resident himself, was the preacher for the morning. He started preaching from Matthew 12:33-37. It was about trees and their fruit. In the judgment, every tree was going to have to give an account of their fruit. It was a short message, which was good because four of the members of the congregation had gone to sleep, and one of them was snoring pretty loudly. Sarah tried hard not to laugh. When it was over, she stayed around visiting and helping them get back to their rooms. One particular lady captured Sarah's heart. Her name was Lucille. She started sharing her story with Sarah. She had grown up poor but had fallen in love with a rich man, whom she married, much to the chagrin of his family. She had been a wing-walker, which was a show girl who dressed in fancy dresses and went up in the airplanes and walked out on the wings during air shows. Wing-walkers did not have the best reputation and Lucille loved men. She loved a number of men and soon found herself pregnant. She would have lost her job, if not for her Harry. He loved and married her, pregnant and all. He loved her so much, he didn't seem to mind that the baby wasn't his. She and Harry had loved to party, till her baby was born. It was a boy and she named him Timothy. She soon learned he had a birth defect and was mongoloid. Lucille was so upset and thought God was punishing her for her wild life. She met another young mother at the doctor's office, who had a baby with the same problem and they became good friends. Her new friend was a Christian and she just loved Lucille to God. Soon Harry became a Christian, too, and they had three more healthy children of their own. Timothy died at the age of twenty-five, but he was the biggest blessing God could have sent them. Timothy had given them years of joy and had led them to Jesus.

Sarah loved Lucille's story. She loved Lucille's openness and how she didn't let the shame of who she had been define who she was now. She had been a bad tree, who became a good tree that produced good fruit. She reminded Sarah of Rachael. She would have to tell Lucille her own story one day. *Thank you Lord, for sending me to these beautiful people. You knew I wanted to serve and be a blessing, but You sent me to people who blessed me.*

She was late to church because of her long visit with Lucille. When Jonathan asked her where she had been, she told him she had been visiting with angels. He just looked at her in wonder. "You are weird, you know?"

"Yes, I know!" Sarah said with a huge smile.

She told him all about it later. He laughed at her description of the service. It made him want to go with her, but he worked with the 11-year-olds during that time.

20

November had arrived and with it came the crisp air of fall and the promise of winter. At school, Sarah had a new challenge, or *another* challenge. Sarah had been over the leave-the-class-and-puke-stage of her pregnancy which had lasted longer than she had hoped. She wasn't the only one who noticed. Jessica walked out of class behind her that morning.

"Not throwing your guts out anymore? I hope there's nothing wrong with the baby. So many girls your age miscarry." Sarah didn't know how to respond. She knew that Jessica was doing everything she could to get to Sarah. Maybe Jessica wanted a showdown. Sarah didn't know, all she knew is that God had touched her heart for Jessica and she would never get to her if she told her off. So she opened her mouth and let God speak.

"I guess I'm through with that part. Sure am glad. By the way, I like your shirt."

Sarah was as shocked as Jessica at what she had just said and didn't wait to see Jessica's reaction; she turned to go down the hall to Biology. *Thank you Lord, for giving me an answer that was kind and not harsh. I could have never done that without You!*

When she walked into Biology, Tyrone took one look at her face and asked her why she looked so thrilled.

"You looked like you just swallowed the canary."

"What?" Sarah asked smiling.

She knew what he meant, but loved his explanations.

"My Gramma used to always say that to us if we had just done something we weren't supposed to, and we thought we had gotten away with it. Usually we had swallowed the cookies instead of the canary."

"Well, I didn't swallow the canary or the cookies, but I think I might have done something good."

She explained what happened and Tyrone just listened. "So now you want to kill her with kindness?"

"Well, I just want God to love her through me."

"That will kill her flesh all right. Way to go, little mama! I like that; God likes that!" Tyrone said with his big smile.

"Thanks, I'm giving God all the credit because, believe me, that was not what my flesh wanted to say to her," Sarah said assuredly.

That night still basking in the small triumph of the morning, Sarah dug into her homework. She needed to do some Pre-calculus problems but she couldn't seem to keep her mind focused enough to figure them out. She had never had trouble concentrating in the past, but that had been before the rape. She finally gave up and decided to take out the paper and do an exercise her counselor had given her. Sarah had told her counselor that she needed help in forgiving Jason. First, Dr. Jane said she was to write an indictment letter that would not be mailed. In it she was to list every accusation against Jason. Then she was to go down the list and forgive him for each thing on the list one by one and follow Jesus' example when he prayed, "Father, forgive them, for they know not what they do."

Sarah's Story

So Sarah wrote "Indictment against Jason" at the top of her page. Then she started her list.

1. Lied to me in a text
2. Trapped me in the house
3. Wouldn't take "no"
4. Hurt my body
5. Terrified me
6. Robbed me of my virginity and my peace
7. Made me endure the humiliation of a being examined for proof
8. Ruined my reputation
9. Got me pregnant
10. Ruined my future
11. Took away my dream of wearing a white wedding dress
12. Gave me nightmares
13. Ruined my dreams of going to the prom
14. Took away my ministry with kids and young girls
15. Made me an outcast
16. Led to my mother's death
17. Made it hard to do my school work because I can't concentrate.
18. Ruined my style. There are no cute pregnant clothes.
19. Took away my chance of making the basketball team

By the time Sarah had finished her list she was more angry than she had been when she started it. She was also exhausted. *I think this is going to take a little more time.* Sarah thought as she climbed into bed. At least she had gotten started.

21

During football season, Rachael spent most Friday nights with Sarah. They would go together to the game if it was at home. Jonathan was the quarterback, even though he was just a junior. Their team was on their way to State. Joey sometimes came with Rachael to spend the night. Corbin and Joey had developed a special bond. They spent many hours in the game room playing Ping-Pong and other games, or outside playing catch or soccer.

Sarah had talked her dad into getting Rachael a cell phone of her own and paying the monthly bill. Corbin didn't mind.... he would do anything to help Sarah and Rachael's friendship, which was a gift from God. When they went to buy it, the salesperson, who was also the manager, insisted on putting Rachael on their family plan.

"So now it's official. You're in my family!" Sarah told Rachael.

They high-fived each other. "Yay!" Rachael said.

Now they could talk everyday after school and discuss their day. They prayed for each other and exchanged helpful scriptures they had found. Sometimes they spent hours just studying the Bible together. Sarah had never had a better friend, one that loved Jesus as much as she did.

Rachael's mother was also doing better. Crystal met regularly with her mentor from the church. She continued to attend weekly "Celebrate Recovery" meetings and her heart was slowly thawing.

One night after supper, Rachael and Sarah were on the phone reading together about the crucifixion. Sarah was reading out loud, "Jesus looked up to heaven and prayed to his Father, 'Lord, forgive them, for they know not what they do.'"

Sarah paused and asked Rachael. "Do you think Jason didn't know what he was doing?"

"I think he knew what he was doing, but had no idea the outcome of his actions and how damaging they would be. He was just totally selfish." Rachael answered with a little anger in her voice.

"Yeah, the Jews knew they were killing Jesus, but because of their jealousy, they couldn't see the facts right before their eyes. Jesus did so much good for people. He healed people, forgave people, fed people and was the greatest teacher. He lived what he taught. The religious people were just spiritually blind; they couldn't see it. I guess Jason's sin and his refusal to deal with his issues made him spiritually blind also. It is just hard for me not to take it personal. Somehow Jesus was able to do that." As Sarah talked it out, God began to open her spiritual eyes. Her unforgiveness had made her blind also.

Sarah burst into tears. She knew what she needed to do. She started praying out loud.

"Lord, I don't want to hold this bitterness in my heart any longer. Please forgive me and set me free from this hatred and unforgiveness. I give it to you and I don't want to come back here again. I free you to do a work in Jason and restore him as you are doing in me. And Lord, please help my dad to be able to forgive too."

"Boy, I bet the devil's not happy now!" Rachael said excitedly.

"No, he's not."

That night Sarah took out her list and placed her hand over it. *Lord, you are going to have to help me with this list.* Then she started with number one. Even though it was extremely difficult, Sarah started praying for them one by one, asking God to forgive Jason for each indictment and forgiving him because he didn't know what he was doing. By the time she was finished she was heaving in despair. She remembered that her counselor had told her forgiveness has to do more with you than the other person. She encouraged her to do this for her...not for Jason. *Okay Lord, I said it, even though I don't feel it. You are going to have to give me the feelings.*

Sarah took out a fresh piece of paper and with a shaking hand she wrote Jason.

> Jason,
>
> I hope that you are doing well in Teen Challenge. I pray that you have found the forgiveness that God wants so much to give you. I just wanted you to know that I have forgiven you for what you did. My prayer is that you be healed in your heart and be able to walk with God and allow him to turn all this for good.
>
> Sarah

It was sweet, short, and to the point, which was what Sarah wanted. She felt free and light...even joyous! She hadn't realized how heavy unforgiveness could be. Now that she had written the letter, what was she supposed to do with it? *Lord, what now?*

She heard the Holy Spirit say, "Don't send it; just keep it. I'll let you know what to do."

Okay, but you might want to get me to do this while I'm willing. I might change my mind.

She heard this answer: "Trust me."

Sarah went downstairs and found Corbin in his study. She presented her letter to him for his approval.

"So, what do you think?"

Corbin slowly read the letter and with tears in his eyes he responded,

"I'm proud of you. Do you want to mail it? His dad gave me his address."

"No, I don't think I'm supposed to mail it," Sarah said. "I think I'm supposed to wait... for some reason. I have no idea why."

"Okay, we can put it right here in my desk drawer. Writing it took courage. I'm proud of you."

"Thanks, Daddy."

22

Sarah woke up early on Sunday morning and looked out her window. The leaves had all fallen off the trees and they stood naked and exposed to the elements which was how Sarah felt at times.

The day was cold and damp and though Sarah would have loved to curl up in her window seat and wrap up in a blanket, she knew she needed to get to the nursing home early. She had planned to go early to talk to Lucille.

Even though Lucille was eighty-eight and her body weak and frail, her mind was as sharp as a tack. She was there, of course, so Sarah asked her if she could talk to her. Lucille brightened up with delight. Sarah told her everything. She might as well. Lucille was too old to tell her story in bits and pieces...She might go to heaven before she finished. Sarah tried to give her the condensed version—the Cliff Notes. Lucille took it all in, with a few "Oh's" and "Oh My's" throughout the saga.

"So that's my story and that is why I'm seventeen and pregnant!"

"That is quite a story, young lady. God has blessed you with wisdom beyond your years. I have learned that circumstances don't define who we are; what we do with them does. You have used your difficult circumstances to bless God and

Sarah's Story

others. You remind me of Job. No one understood why all those horrible things had happened to him, but the way Job reacted to it was very important in the spirit realm. His whole trial was really a showdown between God and Satan and Job was the pawn. Job helped bring the victory to God. That is what you are doing. I'm very honored to have found you."

Sarah teared up and hugged Lucille. "I love you, Lucille. You always know how to make me feel better."

"I do have a question for you, Sarah. I could tell by the way you told your story that you are having a hard time feeling like you have forgiven Jason."

"I am. How should I feel? How do I forgive someone who purposely caused so much pain to me and my family and feel good about it. It is hard to do."

"Yes, it is. I'm sure it was hard for my Harry to forgive me for all the men I had been with, but he did. Forgiveness is a choice. It doesn't always come with feelings you can trust. Sometimes you have to do it by faith, like you did. The feelings will come later. I can say that because I have lived it."

Sarah knew she had. "That helps. I guess I am waiting for some euphoric feeling to let me know I've forgiven him."

"You know what really helps you forgive someone?"

"No, what?" Sarah asked moving in closer like Lucille was about to give her the secrets of life.

"You start praying for them—for God to bless them."

"Bless them? Bless Jason? I thought I should be praying a curse down on his head or something. I definitely never thought of praying for God to bless him."

Lucille smiled. "What would bless Jason the most?"

"That's easy. If he got saved." Sarah, all of a sudden, realized she didn't know if she wanted Jason to get saved. Then God would have to love him. *Now that's stupid! I know God loves him, but...but...* She couldn't even admit that she wished God didn't love Jason. Sarah was seeing herself in a mirror she didn't like.

Sarah's Story

Lucille had waited for Sarah to think about it for a moment, then said, "Do you think you could pray that for him...now, out loud?" Lucille knew she was asking a lot from Sarah, but she also knew Sarah was mature and could handle it. At least she hoped.

Sarah breathed in deeply and said, "I think so." She bowed her head and said, "Lord, you know how I feel, but in spite of that, would you save Jason?"

She looked up at Lucille and said, "My heart was not there, but I said it."

"That's a start. Now, I want you to pray that daily and see what God does to your heart. This is not about Jason as much as it is about you. You don't want to carry bitterness and resentment around with you your whole life. You will look like me at 40!"

Sarah laughed. "You're beautiful, Lucille."

"So are you! And I want you to stay that way."

"Okay, I'll do it because you asked me to."

"That's enough for me."

So now Sarah could add "God, save Jason" to "God, help me love Jessica." at the end of her prayers.

"I do have something else I would like your advice about. I have this, uh, friend, no, she's more like an enemy named Jessica. She hates me because she used to go with Jonathan and I must be a threat to her, or something. Anyway, I am trying to reach out to her and be her friend but the more I try, the worse it seems to get."

"Well, the Bible tells us that we are to love our enemies and do good to those who spitefully use us. That is a hard thing to do, but it wouldn't tell us to do it if it weren't possible. It also says that it is God's kindness that leads us to repentance. Let's pray that God gives you some creative ways to be kind to her."

"That sounds great!" Sarah said hopefully.

Sarah's Story

Lucille prayed that very thing and about everything else Sarah had told her about. Lucille believed in praying specifically so God would answer specifically. They were running late to their service in the nursing home, but Lucille still covered every jot and tittle.

At the service, Charlie was a little "disoriented". Charlie had alzheimer's, and today he thought he was at a dance. He kept trying to get Sarah to waltz with him. She finally gave in and danced with him to the hymn, "Are You Washed in the Blood?" If only the people at school could see her now. The song leader seemed amused. Lucille tried to stifle a giggle. Sarah shot her a look of disapproval. They both had to control their desire to burst out laughing.

The sermonette was from John 11 about raising Lazarus from the grave. Lazarus was Jesus' dear friend and even though Jesus knew Lazarus was really sick, he waited until Lazarus was dead. When he got there, it was the right time, because God wanted to do more than heal another person, he wanted Lazarus to rise from the dead. Sarah thought of her "friend" Jessica. Maybe God wanted Sarah to wait patiently till God prepared the right time to raise Jessica from her death. She left encouraged. Sarah thanked Lucille for listening to her and helping her know what to do. Lucille thanked her for sharing her story. She told her it was the first time in a long time she had felt useful. *How sad*, Sarah thought. *Lucille has so much yet to give. Thank you Holy Spirit for bringing me this wonderful yet fragile person into my life.*

23

Rachael couldn't spend the night Friday because they were going to go visit her mom. It would be the first time they had seen her since her incarceration. Rachael was a little nervous, but excited to see her mom and show her her own change. Rachael had even gotten her granny to start going to church with her and Joey. They had found a small church that was walking distance from their house. It was full of college kids since Ruston is the home of Louisiana Tech University. She had drawn the attention of the worship leader, Luke Thomas, who was a sophomore at Tech.

Rachael looked and acted much older than she was. She had lived a life that had caused her to mature young...very young. He was a very cute, blonde-haired, blue-eyed musician. He was funny, mysterious, and very strong in his faith. He was perfect for Rachael.

They weren't formally dating, but he made sure he talked to Rachael every Sunday and Wednesday night. She was wary at first but his guitar won her heart.

"It's hard not to like a guy with a guitar." Rachael told Sarah.

School was getting better for Rachael, too. With the combination of her growing faith, Sarah's love and friendship and now the confidence Luke's attention gave her, she was becoming more outgoing. She met two girls at church, who accepted Rachael into their circle. She still missed Sarah, but she was blooming where God had planted her. Sarah was so proud of her.

Since Rachael's mom had never been very affectionate or loving, Rachael didn't know how this visit was going to go. She and Sarah had prayed about it on the phone and Sarah had told her to love her mother unconditionally. Rachael was prepared to do that. They walked into the room where they allowed the family to visit the inmates. Her mom was already there waiting. The minute she saw Joey and Rachael, Crystal jumped up and practically ran to hug them. Her face shone. Rachael could hardly believe this new person was her mom.

"Hey, mom, how have you been?" Rachael acted a little shocked. All her mom could do was hug them and tell them that she loved them and was so happy to see them. There were tears shed by all of them. She assured them she was doing fine. She talked about her sessions in her Celebrate Recovery group and how God had saved her. Rachael was beside herself. Joey told her all about his new school and living with Granny. Granny had hugged her daughter, too, but with a little more restraint. There were many years that needed healing. Crystal thanked her mom for taking care of her kids.

"When I get out, we are going to be a family again," her mom said. Rachael couldn't believe what God was doing in her family. She remembered what Sarah had said: that God can change anyone.

That weekend Sarah and her dad had been asked to have supper with Phil and Julie Johnson. Phil and Corbin were partners at work. Sarah had never spent time with the Johnson's, so she wasn't expecting much. The Johnson's were a really nice couple. They met at the Olive Garden and after they had ordered, Mr. Johnson and Corbin started talking about work. Ms. Johnson turned to Sarah and asked her how school was going. They talked for a while about nothing important until she started talking about her daughter, Hannah. Mr. and Ms. Johnson had adopted Hannah when they found they couldn't have children. Ms. Johnson had been sexually abused as a child which had ruined her for conception. Sarah couldn't believe Ms. Johnson was being so open, but then Sarah was seventeen and pregnant so this must have made her feel comfortable sharing so intimately. Hannah was now twenty-eight and married to Drew, the only boyfriend she had ever had. They would be going to Guana, Africa to be missionaries in April. Hannah and Drew were trying to get pregnant and start a family. Sarah had always dreamed of going to Africa on mission trips. Sarah loved her story. When it was time to leave, Ms. Johnson told Sarah that she would enjoy having her over when Hannah came to town so they could meet. Sarah said she would love to and they left.

Sarah had to stop by the grocery store for some items they needed so Corbin went on home. When she pulled into her driveway, Corbin was outside visiting with a woman...it was Lady G! Sarah could tell by her dad's body language that he was extremely uncomfortable about her being there and extremely excited about Sarah pulling up. Sarah was scrambling for a way out for her dad. *Holy Spirit, help!*

"Hey dad, I really need to talk to you. Oh, hi!" she said, turning her attention to Lady G.

"Hi! You must be Sarah! I've been hoping I'd meet you! Aren't you...." She stuttered when she saw Sarah's stomach. There was no doubt Sarah was pregnant. She was so small everywhere, except for the round ball in her belly.

"Cute!" She recovered. It was all Sarah could do not to laugh. How could someone with her propensity to know everything about her dad, have missed the fact that his daughter was pregnant? She must have been so busy learning about her dad that she missed this small detail.

"It's nice to meet you, but I'm sort of in the middle of an emergency, and I really need to talk to my dad. I hope you understand," Sarah said, making it to her dad's side as fast as she could.

"Oh, sure, of course! I hope everything is all right?" she asked with curiosity.

"Thanks, it will be." Sarah said, grabbing her daddy's arm and walking him inside.

"Goodbye," Sarah said over her shoulder.

"Goodbye," Corbin said as he stumbled in the door. They left Lady G standing in the driveway.

"Thanks!" Corbin told Sarah.

"What was that about?" Sarah demanded. "How does she know where we live? And... what is she doing here?"

"She *said* she just *happened* to be in the neighborhood," Corbin said, rolling his eyes.

"I was outside vacuuming my car out when I looked up and she had pulled in. I thought about diving into my car and closing the door, but I figured that would look a little obvious." They both laughed as they tried to picture him doing that.

"Thanks for being my knight in shining armor and saving me." Corbin quipped.

"Anytime. You'd do the same for me." Sarah said, turning to walk upstairs.

24

Jonathan loved to embarrass Sarah, so he would do random things he found funny. One day, at lunch, Sarah was eating with her friends when Jonathan slipped up behind her and said in a disguised voice, "Lady, there is a weight limit in this cafeteria and we notice that you exceed the limit, so we're going to have to ask you to drop your apple and leave before the floor caves in." Sarah's friends cackled and swooned while Sarah turned and said, "You have no idea who you are dealing with. I'm pregnant and mean and if you don't want an apple down your throat, you better go pick on someone your own size." Sarah said, playfully grabbing her apple like she was about to throw it at him.

"Leaving. Thought you might need something to get your blood pumping today." Jonathan grinned as he walked back to his table of friends.

It was a thoughtful gesture on Jonathan's part. He was always looking for ways to show Sarah that he was proud to be associated with her. What Sarah failed to see was that when Jonathan walked over, Jessica was in the table in front of Sarah's and Jessica thought Jonathan was walking over to talk to her. She had even told her friends so. When he walked around her table to get to Sarah, Jessica was embarrassed and scorned. She was determined to get back at Sarah. The truth was that Jonathan didn't even see Jessica sitting there. He was too intent on sneaking up on Sarah.

The next day came with a chilling wind to match Jessica's cold heart. The temperatures had dropped to the low thirties, which is biting cold in Louisiana because it is a damp cold. Sarah wore a poncho to keep warm. She had a doctor's appointment that day at ten, so she had planned to attend her first period class and half of her second period. She hated to miss any school. Jessica was on the warpath. She had not appreciated being scorned the day before and she was out for blood. She walked up to Sarah before school and said, "I guess you think you can hide your stomach with that poncho. Let me guess...Jonathan's the father of your baby, isn't he?"

Sarah was so shocked by her accusation, it took her a moment to respond. Jessica took that pause as a "yes" and went with it.

"I thought so. Are you going to make him marry you?"

With that Jessica stormed off before Sarah could find her voice. The bell rang and Jessica made sure there was no way for Sarah to be able to talk to her before or after class.

Jessica talked with her friends about Sarah all through class. Sarah could feel her knives. Finally, the bell rang and Sarah escaped to second period.

Sarah remembered her prayer with Lucille. They had prayed that God would give her creative ways to be kind to Jessica. *How can I be kind to someone like her, God? She is vicious and mean and hateful and...okay, I get it. This is an attack from the devil because of what I prayed. So Lord, help me know what to do.*

She rounded the corner and entered Biology.

Tyrone...such a welcome change! Tyrone was talking to a girl next to them when Sarah walked in. He turned around and whistled. "Whew, you got big over the weekend. What did you eat, a whole watermelon? I'm going to have to start calling you 'big momma' instead of 'little momma.'" Only Tyrone could say something like that and get away with it.

When Sarah couldn't come up with her usual laugh, Tyrone knew he had said the wrong thing.

"I didn't mean it. You look great...not even pregnant." Tyrone said, trying to dig himself out of his hole.

Sarah was tempted to laugh, but was too upset to even come up with a smile.

"No, it's not that. Jessica thinks that Jonathan is the father and I didn't even have time to defend him. Before this class is over, it's going to be all over the school. What do I do?"

"Uh..." Tyrone was not prepared for that information. "You want to know what my Gramma always tells me?"

"Yes, this would be a great time to have some of your Gramma's wisdom."

"She always says, 'Tyrone, when people say lies about you, just let God bring the truth out. He'll do it in a way that no one can argue. Then, the truth will set you free!'" When Tyrone got to the last sentence he raised his fist like he was proclaiming freedom to the captives. He was very convincing. Sarah couldn't help thinking Martin Luther King, Jr. would be proud of him, just now. She had to smile.

"Thanks, that helps," Sarah said, letting it sink in.

Sarah understood the wisdom of letting God be her defense. If she told Jessica the truth, she wouldn't believe her anyway, but God could prove it in a way Jessica had to believe. Sarah thought about it till it was time to go to her doctor's visit. Right before she left she whispered to Tyrone teasingly. "You better pray I haven't gained too much weight."

He bantered back, "I better fast and pray, since you obviously didn't....fast, I mean."

Sarah hit him on the arm and left smiling. She *did* pray all the way to the doctor's office, but not about her weight. She prayed about Jessica. In the waiting room, she searched "lies" on her Bible App. After reading several verses about those who lie, she realized that God hates lies and the people who bring false witness. Next, she searched "truth" and found a great promise in Psalm 31 which became her prayer.

Lord, I trust in you. Let me never be disgraced. Save me because you do what is right... For the good of your name, lead me and guide me. Set me free from the trap they set for me, because you are my protection. I give you my life. Save me, Lord, God of truth. Then she added, *Please, Lord, save Jonathan's reputation.*

She felt God's peace and assurance that He was strong enough to protect her and Jonathan–and even Jessica. She felt sorry for Jessica, who seemed so eaten up with bitterness and pain. Sarah didn't want to see Jessica pay the price for all her unkindness.

Back at school, Sarah checked in and went to her English class, which was already started. She passed a room and saw Tyrone sitting in his desk by the door. She held up three fingers and mouthed, "Three pounds!" Tyrone acted like he had been hit in the face with surprise. Sarah laughed out loud. She heard the teacher call Tyrone's name and hoofed it around the corner.

All through the day, Sarah looked for repercussions about what Jessica had said, but she couldn't see any. It didn't seem like she told *anyone. Maybe she was afraid to bring Jonathan into the picture since he probably would fight back and Jessica wouldn't want to become his enemy. Thank you, Lord. You saved me from the trap that the devil tried to set for me.*

25

Sarah couldn't wait until Sunday to talk to Lucille so she decided to go visit her Thursday, after school. Sarah still went to her counselor every two weeks, but she had a question that needed Lucille. Lucille was in her own room, sitting at her small table, writing a letter. She was writing to her daughter, Anna, who lived in Washington with her husband, Todd, and their son, Walter. Lucille was "old school" and wanted her daughter to have a written account of her life, so Anna could read it to her grandson after she was gone. Every letter had new memories of Lucille's life as she recalled them.

Lucille's room wasn't dark and depressing like many of the rooms at the home. She had a large corner room with her own furniture from home, except for the bed, which was a hospital bed. She had custom-made pinch-pleated drapes on the window, and a birdcage for her canary in front of the window. There were plants everywhere and plenty of framed pictures of her family. Scripture was everywhere: on plagues, in frames, sitting on stands, or just written on pieces of paper and taped to the mirror. There was a small refrigerator disguised as a plant holder covered with a hand towel and a big recliner draped with a green slipcover. On the opposite wall was a table and two chairs where Lucille was sitting. She offered Sarah the chair opposite her. Her Bible was on the table, opened where she had been reading.

Lucille was thrilled to hear about how Sarah was handling Jessica. She agreed that God had stopped the mouths of the hungry gossip lions.

Jessica was not what Sarah came to talk about. Sarah wanted to ask Lucille about love.

"Is it possible for a seventeen-year-old to be in love?" Sarah wanted to know.

"Of course it is. You're old enough to have a baby, aren't you?"

"Well, I guess so...but I feel so young and awkward and there is so much I don't understand," Sarah reasoned.

"Sarah, you *are* young and awkward, but you have the spirit of God in your heart. You have allowed him to mature you and because of that, you are more mature than some sixty-year-old people I know. Jesus is the one who gives us wisdom. Remember, God chose Mary, who was a few years younger than you, to be the mother of Jesus. I'm sure she felt the same way you do now—too young and totally unworthy. Love starts small, but with time it grows and matures as you do. If this is love between you and Jonathan, it will grow and mature. If not, then, it will die like it did between Jonathan and Jessica."

"That's true. I guess I never thought about it like that. I just look at what my parents had and I know that Jonathan and I don't have that," Sarah mused.

"Of course you don't. That takes years of living and growing together."

"I know I'm not ready for marriage. I don't want to do that until I know it's the right time." Sarah trailed off in thought.

"So it's not crazy to talk about falling in love at my age?" Sarah said, more as a statement than a question.

"That depends on who's saying it. You and Jonathan—no, because it is obvious God brought y'all together. Certainly not all 17-year-olds are as mature as you two. So not all seventeen-year olds are mature enough to fall in love—maybe in *lust!*"

Sarah giggled.

"So have you thought about what you are going to do once you have your baby?" Lucille asked, changing the subject.

"No, when I first became pregnant, God gave me the story about Hannah and Samuel. Hannah gave her baby to the Lord and that's what I've done. Now, I'm waiting for his instructions. So far I either haven't heard, or He hasn't said. He knows he needs to speak really loud to me for me to hear." Sarah said with a smile.

Lucille chuckled. "I'm the same way. That sounds like a good plan."

They talked on until Sarah noticed what time it was, and knew she needed to go. She hugged Lucille and left with a grateful heart.

On the way home, Sarah started crying and couldn't stop. She was so thankful to have Lucille as a surrogate grandmother, since she had none of her own, but she missed her mom. Her mom was the one she should have been asking these questions. There were so many things she still needed her mother to teach her.

That night Sarah found the part in 2 Timothy 1 where Paul was writing to Timothy, who was his young mentee. Paul was praying for Timothy that his tears be turned to joy. He reminded him of the faith of his grandmother, Louis and his mother, Eunice, that now he saw alive in Timothy. He told Timothy to stir up this gift of God, which had been passed down through these women's prayers to him. Then he gave Timothy one of Sarah's favorite verses: "For God has not given us the Spirit of fear, but of power and of love and a sound mind." *Lord, help me to stir up the gift of my mom's faith and my grandmother's faith and not let fear and self-pity hold me back. And, help me*

Sarah's Story

love Jessica. And, please save Jason. This had become her formal closing of every night's prayer like "in Jesus' name".

It was nearing the end of November, and Sarah was beginning to feel a reprieve from drama till she walked into English class. They had begun to study *The Scarlet Letter*. It was difficult, in Sarah's condition, to discuss the life of a woman who became pregnant back in the 1800s—a time when an unmarried pregnant woman got shunned for adultery.

Sarah could relate even though she was in the twentieth century.

Hester had to wear a big scarlet "A" on her chest for the rest of her life so that all would know she was an adulterer. Sarah had her own red "A" even though it was invisible.

It turned out the father of Hester's baby was the minister who helped condemn her. Sarah's was the minister's son who wasn't here to vouch for her.

Hester's minister kept his secret for decades until he was dying. He had carried the guilt and shame his whole life. In his final moments on earth, he confessed to be Hester's lover. After his death, they found that he had a red "A" embedded on his chest.

Hester's once-believed dead husband reappeared the day she was brought out for public shunning. He made her promise not to expose him as her husband, and secretly made her life miserable. Even the baby, which was a girl, grew up under the town's judgmental scrutiny.

There were so many parallels with Sarah's own plight. Sarah was angry that Jason was concealing the scarlet "A" on his chest while she was turned over for public scorn. She wondered if he felt the remorse of Hester's secret lover.

At the end of the unit, Ms. Hamm, her teacher, divided the students into groups. The groups randomly picked a portion of the book to be acted out. They would perform their skits after the Christmas holidays. Sarah's group drew the part where

Hester was brought before the minister and townspeople who judged her "guilty" and gave her the red "A". When Sarah's group met to decide who would play which character, Hester's part came up. Sarah hoped someone would want it since Hester was the leading role. Surely someone in the group wanted to be the star. No, they wanted to make a good grade more. They wanted Sarah to be Hester—but no one had the courage to say it. Instead, they just sat there, waiting for her to volunteer. Steve, the leader finally hinted, "Who can relate to Hester?" Sarah knew they were waiting for her to volunteer.

"Okay, I'll be Hester." relented Sarah. "I definitely can relate to Hester more than any of you." They all laughed nervously.

This is the ultimate humiliation! Sarah thought.

Sarah loved her English teacher, Ms. Hamm. She was young, charming and single. All the guys teased her unmercifully and she took it rather well. She was a great teacher and never seemed to judge Sarah. When she found out which part Sarah's group had drawn, she asked to speak to Sarah after class.

"Sarah, I saw which part your group picked, and that you are going to be playing the part of Hester. I don't know how you feel about it, but if you would like me to swap your part, or be put in another group, I will."

Sarah was touched by her sincere concern.

"It's all right, Ms. Hamm, you don't have to change me. I can do it. I have come to realize that God chooses to use strange things in our lives to make us more like him and this must be one of those things," Sarah said, shrugging her shoulders.

"Well, I just want you to know that I admire your courage. How are you feeling?" She said, not knowing what to say.

"Really big!" Sarah laughed to ease the tension.

Ms. Hamm laughed too. Sarah thanked her and excused herself to her next class.

26

The streets of Monroe were lit up with the colors of Christmas. Stores sang Christmas carols, people became more friendly, and Santa's were sitting everywhere waiting for children to be placed in their laps to give them their requests. Christmas is truly a magical time of year... only it wasn't for Sarah. She usually loved Christmas, but this year she was dreading it. Everything about it reminded her of her mom. Her mom was the one who had given her a love for Christmas. Kathy loved to decorate, cook, shop, and give help to the needy especially during this season. Sarah decided that her mom would want her to enjoy Christmas, but the only way that seemed possible would be to find some way to help others.

The Holy Spirit gave her a great idea. She and Rachael could decorate the nursing home, and Lucille's room for Christmas. Sarah asked her dad if she could use some of their decorations for the nursing home and he readily agreed. He thought they had too many anyway. Sarah lightly decorated her own house, in honor of her mom and had plenty of boxes left.

The first weekend of December, she and Rachael took their decorations to the nursing home. She had talked to Ms. Knight, the administrator about it the Sunday before, who was glad to have someone else do it. The custodian put the tree up and brought them the boxes of the decorations they used every year. Lucille and a few of the other residents came to help. They had a few laughs as they unboxed Santa's with missing arms, mangers without baby Jesus, and Frosty's that sang and danced. Most of the decorations needed to be replaced. Sarah and Rachael then brought in the decorations from Sarah's house and went to work. Jonathan came by after practice to check on them and decided they were having way too much fun, so he stayed and helped decorate the tree. He could reach up much higher than them so decorating the top of the tree became his job.

Gladys, one of the residents, rolled in and when she saw Jonathan, she was instantly 'in love'.

"Who is this good-looking man we have decorating our tree?" She said flirtatiously.

"That 'good-looking guy' is Sarah's boyfriend." Lucille said sternly.

Sarah looked at Jonathan and smiled. "Looks like I have some competition," she said under her breath, trying not to laugh.

"Looks like you do." Jonathan bantered back with a wink.

"You look just like Clark Gable," Gladys cooed.

"Well, fiddle-Dee-Dee, Clark. You sure turn the ladies's heads," Sarah said quoting Scarlet in the movie.

"If you keep teasing me I'm going to be 'gone with the wind'."

"If you do 'I shall faint.'" Sarah said dramatically, still pretending to be Scarlet.

"I could come up with a great line to follow that, but it might get me in trouble." Jonathan said with a mischievous smile.

"Okay, I quit. I can't afford to offend the hired help," Sarah said knowingly.

"You mean I'm getting paid for this? I'll work a little slower if I'm on the clock."

Sarah and Rachael whooped.

That was what she loved about Jonathan. He was smart, funny, and could follow Sarah's jokes. They had a very un-high-school relationship. Neither of them were needy, so they didn't sit together at lunch, and they didn't talk on the phone every night. They both gave each other space and room to have other people in their lives. They also gave God the opportunity to use them with other people. It was a very healthy relationship with total trust.

When they finished their decorating they were pleased. Lucille said it should be pictured in a magazine. Sarah wouldn't go that far. The other residents loved it too. It felt so good to do something for someone who couldn't do it themselves.

"When I come back for my next visit, I'll do your room." Sarah told Lucille. It was time to leave.

27

The youth group was looking for a service project to do for Christmas. Sarah suggested they do something for the foster children who wouldn't be spending Christmas with a family. Because of Rachael's ordeal, she had become more aware of the foster care situation. Caleb thought that was a great idea. They decided to go on Christmas morning and give the children presents and a party. If they went about ten o'clock, most of the teens in the church would be finished with their own families and just be sitting around waiting for lunch. They all agreed that would be a great time.

Sarah was excited to have something to do on Christmas. She talked her dad into coming with her. She didn't want him to be alone on Christmas Day either. The Johnson's had invited them over for a late lunch, so they would have something to do that afternoon.

The youth had worked fund-raisers during the year which they used for the gifts. Jonathan volunteered himself and Sarah to do the shopping for three of them. They had a five-year-old boy named Charlie, a fifteen-year-old girl named Brooke, and a sixteen year old boy named David to shop for.

"Why don't we go visit them first, and find out what they like to do, so we'll know what to get them?" Sarah suggested. She was not afraid of much.

Sarah's Story

Jonathan wasn't afraid as long as he had Sarah with him. So they made a date and went.

The facility was small and crowded. The staff did what they could with the funds they had, but were always glad to have outside help. One of the aides, Daren, took them on a tour of the facility.

The guys slept in one big dormitory with bunk beds. They had a small space for their personal belongings but that was all. They didn't do much in this room but sleep. The girls had a similar room. The kids mainly hung out in the big room where there were couches and a small T.V. The walls were poorly decorated and the whole place needed a facelift.

They were introduced first to Charlie. He was a live wire. He started talking and didn't stop. He was into anything and everything. He rarely slept, which was why no one kept him for long; he wore them slap out. Jonathan was really good with Charlie and they hit it off from the start. They played with an old ball for a while, but Charlie was really into dinosaurs.

Daren pointed out Brooke to Sarah and told her a little about her. Though she had been in many homes, she never stayed anywhere over a month. Daren wasn't sure why, but she knew Brooke's wounds were deep. Brooke, like Rachael, had a mom trapped in drug abuse and didn't know her dad. Sarah decided to talk to her while Jonathan tried to tame Charlie. Sarah and Brooke talked about boys and hair. Sarah thought that the next time she visited, she would bring her flat iron and fix Brooke's hair. Sarah had brought some blue nail polish so they both did their nails.

Their third person was David. David was not so easy. He didn't talk to anyone; he was a total recluse. Sarah asked Brooke if she had ever talked to David and she said, "No, he doesn't talk to anyone. He's creepy."

"Maybe he's not creepy, but shy," Sarah offered, defending him.

"Maybe. I don't know. He just sits and watches everyone," Brooke said.

Sarah got an idea. She remembered in the Bible, how Saul would get an angry spirit, and when David played his music, it would calm him down. She walked over to where Jonathan was pretending to be a Tyrannosaur Rex as Charlie squealed in delight, and asked Jonathan if he would go get his guitar. She told him about her idea and he thought it was worth a try.

Jonathan came back with his guitar over to where David was sitting.

"Hey buddy, mind if I sit with you and sing you a few songs?" Charlie was wanting to sit in Jonathan's lap, but Sarah coaxed him to sit on the floor and listen. When David didn't answer, Jonathan just started playing. David's eyes were transfixed on Jonathan's fingers and his guitar. His face slowly softened. It was awesome to watch. After a few minutes of just playing, Jonathan started to sing. "He is jealous for me. Loves like a hurricane, I am a tree, bending beneath the wind of his love and mercy...Oh, how He loves us; oh, oh, how He loves us..." Jonathan sang on. Sarah noticed a tear in David's eyes. Jonathan noticed, too, and looked up at Sarah and gave a wink. They were both in awe of what the Holy Spirit was doing. Even Charlie calmed down, and listened quietly. Brooke kept painting her toes, seemingly oblivious to what was happening in the spirit, but Sarah prayed that God would move in her heart also. When Jonathan finished his song, David's face seemed to beg for another song so Jonathan went into another and another. At the end of the third song, Jonathan stopped and asked David if he wanted to play. He shied away, but somehow Jonathan sensed he really wanted to try. Jonathan put the guitar in his lap and put David's fingers on the frets and strings and helped him strum. David looked paralyzed in fear so Sarah told him they were going to cover their eyes and not watch, but he needed to just try to play. They all put their hands over their eyes, even Brooke, and waited. Other kids had gathered around and they did the same thing. After a minute of silence, David strummed his first note, then another and another. Jonathan opened his eyes and showed him how to place his fingers for different notes. He strummed some more. Everyone opened their eyes and clapped. David couldn't hold back a grin.

Sadly, it was time to leave because visiting hours were over, so they said their goodbyes and left. On the way home, Sarah and Jonathan couldn't stop talking about what they had witnessed. It was a miracle.

"I know what I'm going to give David for Christmas...my old guitar. It's the one I learned how to play on. We can buy him some beginner books and a new strap and some picks." Jonathan was getting excited.

"Great! Maybe we can get him some worship CDs and a small CD player!" Sarah added.

"That would be perfect!"

"I know what we can give Brooke: nail polish, a flat iron, some Christian-girl magazines and a Bible because she said she didn't have one. I also want to get her an outfit. She commented on what I was wearing. I know it would make her feel special to have something new and not used," Sarah said, excited too.

"I think you're the one who's special," Jonathan said, smiling at Sarah.

"Thanks, so are you!" Sarah said embarrassed.

"Charlie will be easy. Dinosaurs, toys, balls." Jonathan exclaimed.

"And...some P.Js! I can't wait!" Sarah exploded. "Isn't God good to let us be a part of this?"

"He sure is," Jonathan said contentedly, as he turned into Sarah's drive.

28

Sarah had plenty of downtime over the Christmas break to think. One day as Sarah was sitting in her window seat, Samuel kicked her to remind her that he would be coming one day. *I hear you, Samuel. I bet you're wondering what is going to happen once you arrive? That's a great question.* She decided to go back and read about Hannah and Samuel. Hannah gave Samuel up to live in the temple with Eli, the priest. Sarah didn't know any priests, or any temple for that matter, so that was out. She didn't want to just "give" Samuel to anyone unless that was what God wanted. She thought about keeping him, but it never felt right even though it was going to be hard to give him up. He now had fingernails and toenails and was covered with hair. He was about twelve inches long. She kept up with his development on an App she had on her phone. Finally, she decided to ask God about it one more time. *Please Lord, show me who is to raise Samuel. Show me my Eli.* She felt total peace.

It was a balmy sixty-five degrees on Christmas Eve which was typical for Louisiana.

"One thing about Louisiana weather..... if you don't like it, just stick around...it will change." Jonathan had told Sarah when she complained it didn't feel like Christmas.

Sarah's Story

That night there was a candle-lighting ceremony at church. She sat with Jonathan and her dad sat with his friends. The Christmas Eve candle-lighting service had always been her favorite service, but it was going to be hard this year. Sarah was battling over missing her mom, but she was determined to be joyful. Instead, she tried to imagine how Mary must have felt. Mary would be finally settling down in the stable and about to go into labor. *What was Mary thinking? I'm sure that's not how she planned to have her first baby. Instead of her mother and family, she had ewes and cows, and a husband she hardly knew. Instead of the comforts of home and a midwife and nursemaids, she had donkeys and bugs and hay and strange odors... and Joseph.* Thinking about Mary helped her not feel so sorry for herself. Mary was her new role model and hero.

When Jonathan lit her candle she looked up at his face. He looked at her in the candle light, and out of his mouth came, "I love you."

Without a pause, Sarah mouthed back. "I love you." They had never said that before, and though neither of them planned it, neither of them regretted it.

Sarah and Jonathan had promised not to get each other gifts for Christmas. They agreed to give all their money to the kids at the home, which took away the pressure of getting the "perfect gift" for each other. The candlelight service was the best present ever! Between what they saved themselves and what the youth group had raised they had around three hundred and fifty dollars to spend on their three kids.

Sarah and her dad had also elected not to exchange gifts. They both had everything they needed and more, so Christmas morning Corbin got out of bed and whipped up blueberry pancakes while Sarah made homemade blueberry syrup. This was going to be their new Christmas tradition. This was also their effort to form new memories that didn't accentuate the absence of Kathy.

After breakfast, they got ready to go to the party for the foster kids. Sarah had told her dad all about their three kids, so he was looking forward to meeting them. This was much more fun than doing gifts for themselves.

It rained that morning, so when Jonathan came over to ride with them, he was a little down.

"Looks like we won't be playing outside with Charlie and his new soccer ball today."

"It's okay," Sarah said comfortingly. "I always think of the rain as the Holy Spirit raining down on us, so it won't upset me. Let's just see this as God's way of raining down on us his blessings."

"That's a great way to see it. Leave it to you to always find the good in everything! Thanks! I can't wait to give David his guitar!"

The party was supposed to start at ten, but Sarah and Jonathan had promised to arrive early to help decorate. Caleb and his wife, Emily, were already there. They set up the tables and all the Christmas goodies— chips and dips, gingerbread cookies, sliced ham, sausage balls, cream puffs, fudge and punch. It was a feast for a king. As other youth arrived the children came running in chattering and laughing. Their faces were full with anticipation.

Every child would receive three gifts. Jonathan had put the guitar with straps and picks in his old guitar case, so it would only count as one present. Then they had wrapped the books and CD's in a box and the player in another. When the kids came in, David went straight to the corner and settled in. He refused Jonathan's attempt to get him to come to the table to get something to eat, so Jonathan and Sarah took a plate over to him and sat it down beside him. They told him he could take it back with him to his room when the party was over. He looked at the plate with disinterest. Jonathan

Sarah's Story

went over to the tree and brought the two smaller packages for David and handed them to him.

"These are for you, from me and Sarah." Jonathan said enthusiastically as he placed them in David's lap.

David just held them and looked at them. Jonathan looked at Sarah for help.

"Let me help you open it, David," Sarah said as she took the first one and opened it.

"Look! It's a guitar book so you can learn how to play the guitar. And, here are some CD's you can listen to. They have the song Jonathan sang last time we were here."

No response.

Sarah reached for the second one and opened it. "Oooh, it's a CD player so you can listen to your CD's." Sarah thought she saw a little interest. She looked up at Jonathan with a hopeful smile. Jonathan went to get the third present. David's eyes got bigger when he saw the big present. Jonathan started opening it. "But,...here is the best present of all. We figured it wouldn't do you any good to have a book about how to play a guitar, if you didn't have a guitar. So..." He had just taken the last of the paper off.

Now, David was interested. He sat up straight.

"Go ahead and open the case." Jonathan said, showing him how to unlatch the top. Together they lifted the lid and David's whole countenance lit up like a Christmas tree. He didn't know what to do, so he just looked up at Jonathan. Jonathan took the guitar out and handed it to him. He stared at it in utter amazement.

"Well, why don't you try it out?" Jonathan asked, as he helped him hold it right. David started strumming and picking. He had a natural gift. With a little instruction he would be well on his way.

Jonathan worked with him while Sarah went to give Brooke her presents. Sarah had wrapped Brooke's presents with really fancy paper with ribbons and bows like her mom used to wrap hers. Brooke's eyes lit up.

"For me?" she asked, excited.

"Yep, these are for you...from me and Jonathan!"

She opened the magazine first and Sarah explained that she would get one like it every month. It would have her name on the address label. Brooke was excited about that. Sarah had also put some Christian fiction books for girls in with the magazines and a purple Bible. Brooke promised she would read it. Her second gift was a basket full of makeup, nail polish and a straightener—a teen's dream. She loved it! The third gift was the outfit. It was a t-shirt, a hoodie, some cool jeans, socks and some boots. Sarah had left enough of the tags on them to let Brooke know they were all new, without showing the price. She wanted Brooke to feel special and she did. Brooke was so excited about everything. She hugged Sarah and went over to where Jonathan and David were, and hugged him also.

Jonathan told David to practice while he left to give Charlie his presents. They knew Charlie would be so busy eating and playing with everyone else that he wouldn't mind waiting for his presents. Charlie didn't even notice that everyone was getting presents but him. When he saw his presents, he started jumping up and down, clapping and screaming for joy! All Sarah and Jonathan could do was laugh. He was dancing like a maniac, so finally Jonathan grabbed his arm and bent down and told him he needed to calm down and open them. He acted like he hadn't thought about opening them. He threw the paper off his first present, which was a big box of balls: soccer balls, plastic baseballs and plastic bats, a football and a tube of tennis balls. There was a net bag to hold them when not in use. All Charlie could say was, "Wow!" as he ran off, kicking his soccer ball around the room, scattering paper as he went.

Jonathan looked at Sarah, "This would be why I wanted nice weather; so we could go outside."

Sarah's Story

Jonathan ran and gathered Charlie up and brought him back to open his other presents. The next was a basket full of dinosaurs and other plastic animals. Charlie grabbed one of the biggest dinosaurs and was already making dinosaur sounds—whatever that is. He ran to show one of his buddies. Again, Jonathan had to go retrieve him to open his last present, which was a Superman sleeping bag with p.j.'s to match. It even had a cape. He wanted the shirt and cape put on pronto. Then he was off again flying though the paper and people, once again bringing havoc instead of good cheer.

"It's a good thing we only had three presents for Charlie. I'm exhausted!" Jonathan laughed. Sarah agreed.

"I'm sure the staff is going to 'thank us' for this!" Sarah said sarcastically.

Out of nowhere, Superman ran up and enveloped Sarah with a hug and a kiss. "Thank you, Sarah. I love you."

Sarah's heart melted. Then he flew over to Jonathan and did the same to him. Jonathan was trying not to cry as he picked Charlie up, and walked him back over to where David sat strumming on his guitar. Jonathan thought he heard David singing softly but couldn't say for sure; it was very loud and crazy in the room. Jonathan showed him how to read his book and Sarah sat with Brooke until it was time to go. Brooke hugged Sarah and thanked her again.

When Sarah walked over to where Jonathan and David were, David looked up at Sarah and in a deep voice said, "Thank you." Sarah could hardly control her emotions. It was the first time they had heard his voice. All she could get out was, "You're welcome." She looked at Jonathan with amazement.

They told David they had to go, but would be back. David then stood up and awkwardly hugged both of them. He told Jonathan "thank you" also.

As they were walking out they asked the social worker if she had ever heard him speak, and she said she hadn't. She told them that David had been badly abused by his father, and his mother was nowhere to be found. He had been found lying in his own feces in an abandoned apartment building by the police. He was covered with bruises, lacerations, and cigarette burns. He probably wouldn't have made it through the night, if they hadn't found him. That was a year go and it had taken a while to nurse him back to health. That news broke Jonathan and Sarah's hearts. It was a lot to take in, but they knew they had to keep visiting these kids. They decided to talk to Caleb and see if the youth group would want to continue visiting on a monthly basis. As for Jonathan and Sarah, they were going to come back every Sunday afternoon they could.

Corbin had been standing with Caleb and Emily through most of the party observing and helping when needed. Corbin was so proud of his daughter's heart, he had to fight back tears. He truly missed Kathy and he was witnessing her through Sarah. He knew that Kathy would have loved being a part of this.

After cleaning up, Jonathan went back home to his family, while Sarah and her dad went straight to the Johnson's for lunch. Sarah was looking forward to meeting Ms. Johnson's daughter, Hannah and her husband, Drew. The Johnson's lived in a beautiful house on the bayou that looked more like a plantation. The back of their living room was all glassed in so there was a beautiful view of the bayou. Sarah could imagine how beautiful it must look in the spring when the azaleas bloomed. Hannah and Drew were so friendly and seemed genuinely glad to have their company on Christmas. Hannah sat next to Sarah at dinner and ended up in conversation about Hannah and Drew's coming trip to Africa. Sarah was fascinated they would be living in such an exotic place. She admired them for their bravery and commitment. Sarah got up the nerve to ask Hannah if she was pregnant yet. Hannah's face turned ashen and sad.

Sarah's Story

"We just found out I can't have babies," She said quietly.

"Oh, I'm so sorry. I hadn't heard. I just knew you were trying," Sarah bumbled out.

"It's okay. We know God has a plan. He promised me I would have a son and his name would be called Samuel, and he would be instrumental in bringing salvation to his generation," Hannah said matter-of-factly.

Sarah sat stunned. Hannah had just said the exact thing that God had told her over three months ago. Sarah couldn't contain herself. "I have to tell you something," Sarah said, excitedly. She knew God had answered her prayer. She told Hannah what God told her.

"I believe You and Drew are the ones that are supposed to raise my baby," Sarah said, thrilled. She and Hannah both hugged each other and cried tears of joy.

Hannah couldn't believe it. She called Drew over and had Sarah tell him the same thing she had told Hannah. He was overwhelmed as well. Then they called the parents over and told them. There were many tears of joy flowing.

"When is your baby due?" Hannah asked.

"April 8."

When are you leaving for Africa?'

"April 11. We had to get the tickets in advance and they are 'nonrefundable'," Hannah said, a little discouraged. "According to the missionary guidelines, a baby has to be at least three days old, which means your baby has to come by your due date."

"That's perfect," Sarah said, pushing aside what her doctor had told her about how first babies usually don't come on time.

"It looks like God will have to bring this baby right on time!" Sarah said, without missing a beat. Sarah had seen God do too much to get discouraged about a little date.

They all agreed.

On the way home, Sarah looked at her dad and said, "This was a landmark Christmas. I hope mom was watching."

"I'm sure she was," Corbin said with a smile.

29

Sarah couldn't wait to tell Rachael, and Lucille, and Jonathan, and ... Jason. She kept forgetting about Jason, and the fact that this baby was his, too. She needed to tell him... sometime. As she thought about the whole thing, she felt like Joseph when he revealed to his brothers that he was still alive and what they meant for harm, God meant for good. Maybe one day she would share this with Jason. It was how she felt. The devil meant this to harm them both, but God had a higher purpose. It was like God used the devil to do His plan.

Sarah decided to add this news to the bottom of Jason's letter so she went downstairs and got it. She added: *I want you to know that I'm not keeping the baby. I have found a couple that is going to raise him. They are missionaries to Africa.*

That next Tuesday as she was telling Lucille about her meeting with Hannah and Drew, she noticed a blanket that Lucille was working on in a basket with crochet needles and yarn. She had never wanted to knit before, but all of a sudden she did.

"Lucille, what are you knitting?" She asked her.

"Oh, just my umpteenth blanket for another baby. This one will be for my new great-nephew."

"Would you teach me how to knit? I want to make one just like yours for Samuel," Sarah beamed.

"Sure, I would love to teach you," Lucille said, grateful to pass on her love for knitting.

She told Sarah how much yarn to get and where to go to buy it. Sarah was so excited. She was going to be the first high school knitter she had ever known.

30

The holidays were over much too soon for Sarah and before she knew it, she was back in the routine of school. The decorations and beauty of Christmas were replaced with the hope of a better new year. It was also time for the dreaded play in English. Sarah had practiced her part well.

She walked into the room wearing a long dress. The dress accentuated her own baby. She had pinned a huge red "A" on her dress. She was accompanied by Steve, who was bringing her to be judged. Aiden played Rev. Dimmesdale, the father of her child and a boy named Josh played the stranger in the crowd, who was really her husband, believed to be dead until this meeting.

Sarah/Hester sees her husband/Josh in the crowd and has to hide her surprise that he is alive and standing there. Her husband recognizes her and asks Ashley who this woman is and what her crime is. They inform him that she has committed adultery and refused to name her lover. He is full of wrath and jealousy. There are four male students sitting in bar stools behind Sarah who are the judges. The class is the crowd. They are to heckle her and call her names. The group had handed out cards to the people in the class with things they were supposed to say that were terribly harsh. The governor of Salem stood and pronounced her crime and its punishment. Her crime: she has had a baby out of wedlock and she refuses to name the father. Her penalty should be death, but because of the mercy of the court, she is instead sentenced to three hours of humiliation before the town, then forever to wear the scarlet "A" on her chest. The old minister, John Wilson, got up and introduced the younger minister, Rev. Dimmesdale, aka Aiden. Rev. Dimmesdale pleads with Hester to reveal to the crowd who her fellow sinner is and release him from his hypocrisy and sin, since he hasn't the courage to do it himself. She gives a determined, "Never." She knows that no one would believe that their dear Reverend is the father but, most of all, she wants him to take responsibility and to admit it himself. She knows it is the only way of true repentance for him. Since he doesn't have the courage to confess and repent, she refuses to name him. Once he realizes his secret is safe, he unleashes a fiery sermon on the sin of adultery. Hester must stand there and take it. So in this case, Sarah stands and takes Aiden's condemning sermon. He must have gotten it straight from a fire and brimstone sermon, like the famous sermon "Sinners in the Hands of an Angry God." It was the hardest half hour for Sarah and she couldn't imagine how Hester endured it for three. When it was over several girls in the class had tears in their eyes. Ms. Hamm was one of them. They got a red "A" in her grade book, to match the one Sarah wore on her chest.

How did Sarah's group get such a perfect part? Sarah knew only God could have orchestrated it, and He had his reasons. Maybe she couldn't suffer as much as Jesus did, but she could identify with Hester. Sarah had her secret of being raped, which if she would have revealed it, might have exempted her from much of the scandalous talk floating around, but it would have condemned Jason. Instead, she had chosen, like Hester, to bear the humiliation and shame. Sarah didn't wear a physical "A"; only an invisible one which her belly attested to be true. Now she had the opportunity, again in front of her English class, to bear embarrassment and persecution. Certainly, God had to have a plan. It was excruciating for her and for many of her classmates who sensed it was wrong.

God gave her grace to play the part, and she was more than glad when it was over.

January and February were full of schoolwork, basketball games, knitting with Lucille on Tuesdays, and visiting the Children's Home on Sunday afternoons. Sarah tried to go to all of her friend's games and Jonathan's varsity games. Rachael and Luke would drive to Monroe for Jonathan's home games. Sarah loved having Rachael and Luke to sit with. Luke missed high school sports, and loved watching Jonathan play. Jonathan played point guard, which was what Luke had played in high school. Luke would coach him and tease him about his goofs afterwards. They would usually pick up a pizza and take it to Sarah's house. They loved to eat and play games. Corbin would join them when they could pull his arm.

Corbin bought a Ping-Pong table for the game room. Sarah's baby got in the way of her backhand, so she and Rachael watched Jonathan and Luke play. Luke and Jonathan had become great friends, even though there was a three-year difference in their ages. They both shared the same passion for music, sports, and Jesus—not in that order.

Sarah was getting closer and closer to her delivery date. She had stayed in close contact with Hannah.

When she told her doctor about the adoption, he seemed concerned. He tried to warn her again that first babies were usually late, and he didn't believe in inducing, unless the baby was in distress—another one of Dr. Abel's "old school" beliefs. He believed that to bring a baby out before it was ready was like bringing a cake out of the oven half-baked. He liked his babies well done! Sarah knew that God would work it all out. Hannah and Drew were trusting God too.

Hannah asked Sarah if it would be okay if she and Drew recorded themselves reading scripture and talking to Samuel. They could send Sarah the CD, and she could play it at night. That way Samuel could get used to their voices. Sarah loved the idea and readily agreed, so they sent their recorded CD to Sarah. She would listen to their soothing voices every night as she drifted off to sleep. Sarah memorized a ton of scripture through those tapes. As sad as it was going to be to part with Samuel, it was 'off-set' by the excitement of seeing Hannah and Drew receive their promised son.

God, You do all things well.

31

One day, while standing in the lunchroom line with her four friends, Sarah remembered she had left her favorite pen in English. She told her friends she was going back to get it. When she got to the English room, the lights were off, but when she tried the knob, it turned. She went in without knocking because she thought no one was there. That is when she heard sobs. It was Ms. Hamm, sitting at her desk with her head on the desk, crying.

Awkward! What now? "I'm so sorry...I didn't know you were here...uh, I left my pen."

Ms. Hamm looked up, startled, but relieved it was Sarah. "Oh, hi, Sarah."

Sarah couldn't just leave like she didn't care. "Are you okay Ms. Hamm? Is there anything I can do for you?"

"Well...can I ask you something?" Ms. Hamm asked, blowing her nose into her Kleenex.

"Sure," Sarah answered a little confused.

"How did you feel when you first found out you were pregnant?" She asked sheepishly.

So Ms. Hamm is pregnant—and she isn't married.

"Did you just find out?" Sarah asked, cutting to the chase.

Sarah's Story

Ms. Hamm looked at Sarah, wondering whether to confide in a student, then nodded her head 'yes'. "Last night." She needed to tell someone.

"Don't worry Ms. Hamm, if anyone can keep your secret, it's me. I have a few of my own..." Then answering her question, "I felt like someone had hit me in the stomach and I had lost my breath. I was devastated!"

"Yeah, that's just about how I would describe it, too...my parents are going to be so disappointed in me."

I guess you never stop worrying about what your parents think, Sarah thought.

"Well, there is one thing I have learned through all this," Sarah said, rubbing her belly. "Parents eventually get on board. They may be disappointed at first, but they'll forgive you, and be excited before too long. That's what parents do."

"I sure hope so. Thanks for your encouragement."

"Ms. Hamm, God is still the same God he was before you got pregnant, and He will never leave you. He'll always be on your side," Sarah said with confidence. "Believe me, I know."

"Thanks, I needed to hear that," Ms. Hamm said, wiping her eyes and trying to compose herself.

"I'll be praying for you," Sarah said as she was leaving.

"Thank you, Sarah."

Sarah didn't get her pen that day, but she did gain a friend.

Sarah realized she was not the only one with problems. She wondered if the father was involved. *Lord, please give Ms. Hamm courage and grace when she tells her parents, and help them to forgive and support their daughter. Give Ms. Hamm wisdom with all her decisions.*

Sarah's friends were so busy talking, they didn't seem to realize that Sarah had been gone most of lunch. She had to gobble down her food so fast, she didn't have time to talk, which was fine with her. Sarah kept Ms. Hamm's secret. She didn't tell anyone—not even Rachael or Jonathan. She added Ms. Hamm to her prayer list.

The next day, Ms. Hamm had a substitute. She never came back. The substitute teacher explained that Ms. Hamm had some medical problems and wouldn't be able to finish the year. Ms. Hamm had asked the substitute to tell them 'bye' for her and that she was going to miss them. Sarah was sad; she was going to miss Ms. Hamm. She really liked Ms. Hamm and would have loved to talk to her again before she left.

The next day, God gave her a perfect opportunity to be alone with Jessica. Ms. Tanner, her Pre-Cal teacher asked Jessica to take some empty boxes to the office. Jessica would need some help, so Ms. Tanner asked for a volunteer. Sarah's hand went up before she realized it. Sarah knew this had to be the Lord, because the thought of being alone with Jessica scared the pee out of her. Jessica looked as shocked and scared as Sarah was, even though she tried not to show it. Sarah picked up the empty boxes and weakly smiled at Jessica, and together, they walked out of the room. You could have heard a pin drop. Everyone knew what was going on between the two of them, and most of them believed that Jessica was only dating Trey to make Jonathan jealous and get him back. *Now what Holy Spirit?* Sarah knew she needed to seize this opportunity, so she breathed in some air and started talking.

"Jessica, I thought that your idea for the new lunch cards was a great one. I think they'll make a big difference. And... I don't know how to say this but I was praying for you the other night and I felt like God told me to tell you that He wants to bring healing to you." Sarah said with a trembling voice.

Jessica whipped her golden brown hair around so fast and looked at Sarah like she was a foreign object that needed to be exterminated. "Why would you care anything about me?" She said in a cynical voice.

"Because that's who I am. Anyway, I just wanted you to know that I'm here when you need someone to talk to."

"Whatever, Sarah," Jessica said as she rolled her eyes trying to recuperate from Sarah's statement.

They walked on in silence.

They made it back to the classroom, and everyone stared when they walked in. Sarah was used to the stares. She had never thought of herself as being brave, but God was causing her to become just that.

She floated blissfully into Biology. It was so uplifting to be used by God. Tyrone could tell she was exceptionally happy. He had been her counselor her through many episodes with Jessica before.

"Well, don't we look happy! Let me guess...Jessica didn't come to school today?"

"No, it's better than that," Sarah said, and explained what God did. Tyrone listened with a knowing smile on his face.

"Whoa, that was sure bold of you! That is how you 'love your enemies' right into the kingdom of God. Great job, little mama."

"Let's just pray that God touches Jessica's heart and she comes back to Him."

"Okay," Tyrone promised, trying to have Sarah's faith.

Sarah loved Tyrone. He was such a warm Jesus to her. He would always ask about her baby and how she was feeling. He understood pregnancy. Tyrone was the oldest of seven, so about every two years his momma was pregnant. He said that between his aunts and his momma, someone in his family was always pregnant. This made Sarah laugh!

The rest of the week went by without too much drama. Sarah was doing well on her blanket for Samuel. She was over half done. Lucille said she had a real talent for knitting. According to Lucille, not everyone does. That made Sarah feel good. She only worked on it at the nursing home, so she could have Lucille right there to help her when she ran out of yarn or messed up. She also enjoyed the friendship they had formed.

Lucille shared with Sarah all the rejection she faced raising a mongoloid baby: enduring peoples' stares at the grocery store, church, restaurants—everywhere. People just didn't know how to deal with the imperfect. Sarah understood that. Sarah had always been two years older in maturity even though she looked two years younger. Now that she was pregnant, she looked more like a pregnant fifteen-year-old, which just got her more judgmental stares. She hated going anywhere by herself because she felt so vulnerable and unprotected. One day in Target, she overheard a woman say, "I don't know what I'd do if my little girl if she came home pregnant like her." It was hard not to feel ashamed and rejected. Mothers tried to shield their children from her if they saw their kids smiling or looking at Sarah. Sarah just wanted this whole year to be over. *Just a few more months, or weeks!* She would tell herself. *How did Jesus carry the shame of the whole world?*

At the end of every visit, Lucille would always ask Sarah what she could pray with her about. They prayed about Jessica, her relationship with Jonathan, Rachael and Luke, and Rachael's mom, who was doing amazingly better and better, and her pregnancy...but today she wanted prayer for her dad.

"I know it's only been seven months, but I want him to meet a wonderful Christian woman and fall in love again. He's only forty and so good-looking and he needs a companion. I can tell he's lonely."

"That is a very unselfish prayer. Let's pray that God brings him a godly wife...I love this!" Lucille said enthusiastically. She was a hopeless romantic.

That night, Sarah talked to her dad about meeting a lady-friend. She told him that she and Lucille were praying for him to meet someone. He was not as excited as they were about it.

"No one can replace your mom. She was so special—she understood me. She was my soulmate. I just don't think there's anyone else out there that could put up with me, much less love me, like your mother. And, I don't think there's anyone out there I could love like I loved your mother." Seeing the disappointment on Sarah's face, he added, "I appreciate your concern for me. It's very thoughtful...I'm just not ready."

"Well, Dad, you are right. No one will ever replace Mom. I don't *want* anyone to do that. I just want you to have someone to take care of you and love you. I'm not always going to be around and I don't want you to live by yourself."

Then Sarah resigned, 'I'm going to pray about it anyway. Mom didn't come into this world knowing how to make you happy—she had to learn. Someone else can do that too. And, I'm sure God can show you how to love someone back."

"Since when did you become such an expert at raising a dad?" Corbin teased.

Sarah laughed, "Since you needed some help."

Corbin chuckled. Even though he knew his daughter meant well, he just didn't see it happening.

32

Two weeks later, Corbin was standing in the vestibule at church. Lady G had cornered him and was trying to pin him down to a time when he could come to her house for supper or lunch, or breakfast, or brunch...anything. Corbin was wearing down and looking for an escape when he heard his name being called.

"Corbin? Corbin Levine? Is that you?"

Corbin turned to see one of the most beautiful women he had ever seen. She took his breath away. He came to his senses and saw the resemblance.

"Nancy? Is that you? It's so good to see you!" Corbin finally spit out.

Nancy Smith had grown up across the street from him, and they used to be best friends in grade school. They had shared a secret crush on each other off and on during Jr. High and High School. It just seemed crazy to like the guy you played cowboys and Indians with, or the girl who could skip a stone more times than you could. It was too awkward back then...but that was then.

They hugged each other, and started talking and didn't come up for air. Poor Lady G. Corbin forgot she was there, so she took the hint and faded into the sunset...which translates: she sat down behind them where she could watch from

Sarah's Story

a safer distance. She had been dissed for a stunning "blast from the past."

Nancy had married a guy named Ted Williams, she met at college, who had became a criminal defense lawyer. Nancy was an interior decorator. They had a son, Tyler, who was a year older than Sarah. Nancy and Ted had a very good marriage until two years ago when he was killed at his office one night of a gunshot. He was defending a man against a gang leader and was getting close to being able to put him away for life.

Nancy was in West Monroe visiting her sister, Susan, who also attended the First Baptist Church. As the service started, Nancy invited Corbin to sit with them. Corbin had forgotten about Lady G till he was sitting down. He felt a little bad about it...but just a little.

After church, Susan invited Corbin out to their house for lunch. Corbin was on his own since Sarah and Jonathan had plans to drive to Ruston to hang out with Rachael and Luke. They had sat in the back of the church and left when it was over.

Susan had prepared King Ranch Chicken casserole, which is a Louisiana favorite. It was delicious. Afterwards, they sat outside on the porch reminiscing about their childhood.

Corbin remembered the time he and Nancy hid in the bushes waiting for Susan, who was seven years older, to come out of the house with her date. The minute they stepped off the porch, Corbin and Nancy doused them with the hose and ran. They took off around the house to the backyard, over the fence and down the block, laughing the whole way. Susan also remembered that night, because she had mascara running down her face, and her hair was soaking wet along with her clothes. She told the guy she couldn't go out with him and went back inside. She pretended to be mad, but was really relieved because she didn't want to be out with that guy anyway. They had really done her a favor, but she didn't tell that part when she told her parents what they did. Corbin and Nancy were both grounded from playing together for two weeks.

They visited out on the porch another two hours after lunch. Corbin hadn't felt so at home since he had moved to Monroe. He realized how much he missed familiarity. Their whole lives had been thrown up in the air the last few months and it felt like they hadn't landed yet.

Corbin couldn't believe it was almost four o'clock when he looked at his watch. Time had flown and he hated to leave. Nancy was smitten with Corbin. Corbin had always been handsome, but age had made him even more so. He had a confidence and sense of humor that endeared everyone to him. Corbin felt the same way about Nancy. Unfortunately, she was leaving the next day for Austin. They exchanged information and both knew they would meet again...soon.

Corbin drove home in another world. Never in his wildest dreams did he think he would feel this way again. He felt like a teenager, crushing over an old flame. He decided not to share details about his day with Sarah, because he knew his face would give him away. Sarah and Jonathan were supposed to go to the Children's Home after their visit with Rachael and Luke, then back to the church to help Pastor Caleb with something. They wouldn't be home till almost bedtime, so maybe by then, Corbin could calm down and act sensible. All he could think about was Nancy.

Things didn't go quite like Corbin had hoped. Sarah came home earlier than expected. She started right in cross-examining him as she was walking into the house.

"Who was that gorgeous lady you were sitting with at church?" she yelled to her dad from the kitchen.

There was no way she was letting Corbin out easy.

"That was just Nancy," He said as nonchalantly as he could.

"*Just* Nancy? Who's '*Just* Nancy'?" Sarah asked, losing patience.

"Nancy Williams. We grew up together in Bunkie, Louisiana. We're just friends."

Sarah didn't buy that for a minute.

"Just friends?" She could tell by her dad's silly grin that he was not himself. "I think you're *crushing* on Nancy."

"I'm not *crushing* on Nancy," Corbin said, trying to keep a straight face.

"Right," Sarah said, not believing him.

"Is she single? Did you have lunch with her? Are you going to see her again?" Sarah asked.

"Yes, to all of your questions." Corbin said, trying to hold back his joy.

"Yes!" Sarah yelled, not afraid to show hers. "Yes, God!" Sarah said, smiling and walking up to hug her dad. "I'm so glad. God answered my prayer," She said with a wink. "So, when am I going to get to meet *Just* Nancy Williams?"

Corbin couldn't hold it in any longer. He started laughing. "You are relentless...you know?"

"Yes,...And I just want you to know that I approve."

"Well, thank you, miss 'Match.com' I'm glad to have your official approval."

"Oh, it's not official till I meet her."

"Okay. The next time she's in town, you can meet her."

"When is that going to be?" Sarah demanded.

"I don't know, but you'll be the first person I tell."

"Okay. I love you, Daddy. I'm so glad you met Nancy," Sarah said honestly.

Corbin just chuckled. "How was your afternoon?"

"Great! David is actually talking to Jonathan. They are *stuck* together like glue and I'm totally not invited. That's okay. I had a great visit with Brooke, and I'm getting good at making dinosaur sounds, according to Charlie."

They both laughed.

Sarah kissed her dad goodnight and told him to go call his new girlfriend.

Corbin was about to object, but then he realized it *wasn't* such a bad idea.

33

Sarah couldn't get Ms. Hamm out of her thoughts. She asked what her dad what he thought about her writing her English teacher a letter. He thought it was a great idea. He called the school and pulled some strings to get her address.

The kids at school had devised all kind of gossip of why Ms. Hamm had left, from cancer, to eloping, to going to Hollywood to be the next Bachelorette. Sarah tried to stop any rumors that came in her circle of influence. She hated that she didn't get to say goodbye or talk to Ms. Hamm again. She wondered how it went when Ms. Hamm had told her parents.

That night she sat down and tried to write a letter. What was she going to say? She couldn't seem to be able to start. *This is not working...Maybe I should pray about it...a novel thought!* So she did and she waited—nothing! *Okay, maybe I should take out my Bible and find a scripture to get me started.* So, she did. She started searching, which was hard, since she didn't know what she was searching for. She started in Galatians and skimmed through it. She found a great verse for Jessica—Gal. 6:10 "Therefore, as we have opportunity, let us do good to all, especially to those who are of the household of faith." *Lord, give me an opportunity to do something good for Jessica.*

Back to her search. Next she went to 2 Corinthians. It was full of some great teaching, but Sarah decided that her goal was not to preach to Ms. Hamm, but to encourage her, so she turned to the Psalms. She found a great scripture to read to Samuel. She finally found something in Proverbs 2:6-7. "For the Lord gives wisdom; out of his mouth comes knowledge and understanding. He lays up sound wisdom for the righteous; he is a buckler to them that walk uprightly."

Sarah prayed for God's wisdom and remembered James, so she turned to James and started reading. Now, she was ready to start writing.

Dear Ms. Hamm,

I have been thinking and praying for you ever since we talked that day. By now, you have probably told your parents, and they are helping you. I pray this is so. With all my trials of pregnancy, I have learned to love the Holy Spirit and my Bible. One of my favorite books in the Bible is James. It has given me much comfort and wisdom, and I thought it could help you, too. In the first chapter, James talks about how we should be full of joy through our trials, because God is working a greater work in us than we can imagine. Boy, is that hard to do sometimes! I have never thought of myself as brave, but God has given me His strength through this pregnancy and even brought me joy. I pray He will do the same thing for you. James also says that when we don't know what to do, or how to pray, we can ask and God will give us the wisdom we need. I pray that the Holy Spirit will give you wisdom and comfort, too. The Holy Spirit has done that for me. He listens to me and speaks to me all through my day. I couldn't make it without Him. I hope everything works out well for you and your baby.

Your partner in prayer and pregnancy,

Sarah

P.S. Everyone misses you at school! You were my favorite teacher! Rumor has it you either had cancer or you eloped or you moved to Hollywood to the be next 'Bachelorette'! LOL, enjoy the show!

    Sarah read over it and decided it was as good as it was going to get. She folded it, put it in the envelope and stuck a stamp on it. *Lord, please let this letter minister grace to Ms. Hamm, and use me in Jessica's life.* Before she sealed it, she would have her dad read it. Sarah had told him about Ms. Hamm because she knew he could keep their secret. She had come to see the wisdom and safety in getting his opinion.

    Corbin read the letter and gave his approval. The next day Sarah walked out to the mailbox after school to mail Ms. Hamm's letter. The mail had already run, so she grabbed it and put hers in. She thumbed through the mail and stopped in her tracks. There was a letter addressed to her. The return address was Jason—Teen Challenge! Her heart skipped a beat. She took it inside and just looked at it, afraid that if she opened it, Jason might pop out of the envelope. Fear tried to pull her in, but she refused to let it.

This is stupid! He's not in that envelope! She just stared at it, then threw it on the table. *I'll wait till daddy gets home to open it.* She ran upstairs and grabbed her Bible. She read it and prayed till her dad came home.

When Corbin walked in the door, Sarah was waiting. She tried to wait until he at least made it in the door before she told him she had gotten a letter from Teen Challenge. When she told him, Corbin's face went white.

"So, did you read it?" was all he could find to say.

"No! I haven't opened it yet. I was waiting for you. Will you open it and read it first?"

"Sure I will," Corbin said, following her pointed finger to the letter lying on the table.

Corbin slowly opened the letter with his letter opener, obviously bracing himself for what it would say. He read it quietly to himself, while Sarah watched anxiously. When he had finished, he looked up at Sarah and told her that Jason was writing to ask her forgiveness.

"Do you want me to read it to you?" Corbin asked, a little shaken himself, but trying to be strong for Sarah.

Sarah could tell her dad was holding back a tear.

"Yes, I don't think I can." She said, and continued pacing. Corbin cleared his throat and began.

Sarah,

I know it's been a while since you called, but up till then, I wasn't willing to admit what I had done to you or anyone else for that matter. I thought I was entitled to make everyone as miserable as I was. After you hung up, it hit me really hard what I had done and the consequences of my behavior. I had been planning to run away that next night because I hated all the rules and restrictions. When I realized you were pregnant with my baby, it did something to me. I cried that night for the first time in about ten years. My counselor, Steve, was there for me. He talked with me almost all night and I finally gave my life to Jesus. I had never done that before. I hated God, the church, and my dad. All I could see about God was rules and hypocrisy. I now understand, Jesus is not like that. Steve has been mentoring me ever since. I finally got the guts to write you to ask you to forgive me for what I did to you. I know what I did to you was awful. I hate who I was. I don't deserve your forgiveness, but I pray you will one day forgive me. If you need any money for the baby or anything...let me know.

Jason

By the end of the letter, Sarah was sobbing. Her dad held her for a while, as they were both trying to process their feelings.

"Wow, I'm so thankful he found Jesus. This is what we've been praying for. I guess this is why I never was allowed to send that letter I wrote. God has been working in Jason's life and he needed to write the letter first."

Corbin agreed with Sarah. They were both full of emotion. It was hard to go back to that night, but the pain was getting less and less and praying for Jason had brought much healing to both of them.

"That knife in my stomach is not there anymore," Sarah realized.

Corbin sat in silence, then replied as he had the same revelation, "Mine is gone too. Thank God, I didn't want to die of ulcers." He said to add some much needed humor.

"No, that wouldn't do," Sarah laughed.

"I need to respond to this," Sarah said, holding up the letter to God. "Help me do that, God."

"God will give you the right words. Sarah, this whole thing is bigger than us. That's all I can say."

"I agree."

That night Sarah read the story of Joseph where his brothers sold him into slavery. They were malicious to him. They mocked and ridiculed him, took his special coat from him, and wanted to kill him. They would have if it hadn't been for Rueben who persuaded them instead to sell him into slavery. Joseph spent thirteen years in different pits and jails. He was falsely accused of defiling Potipher's wife and forgotten about by the cupbearer. When Joseph finally got to see his brothers, he had totally forgiven them. He had come to realized it had been God's plan all along. God had to get him to Egypt to be the second in command just so he could save his family. Even if they didn't deserve it–they were God's children. That was her life in a nutshell, only she didn't want to spend thirteen years in a pit of unforgiveness and pain. She wanted to be healed and helping others.

Lord, thank you for reminding me that your forgiveness knows no bounds. There is no sin you can't forgive except to blaspheme the Holy Spirit, whatever that means. Help me write this letter.

Sarah took out a piece of paper and began to write.

Jason,

I got your letter today. I was moved by what God has done in your life. I want you to know that I did forgive you and am continuing to forgive and heal. I pray that you can forgive yourself too and that you will continue to grow in your faith. I know your parents will be glad, too. There is nothing you can do for the baby. I have decided to give him to a Christian couple named Hannah and Drew to adopt. They are missionaries to Africa. God is going to do great things through him. His name is Samuel.

Sarah

Sarah looked at the letter and cried, but this time for freedom. It felt so good to know that God was with her and that what the devil planned for her hurt ended up being for their good.

She never mailed her other letter, but kept it as a reminder of her commitment to forgive Jason.

34

At school, things were getting better. Jessica seemed to be warming with the weather. She hadn't been antagonistic since their walk to the office, and Sarah had smiled at her a few times. Jessica just stared back then turned away. Sarah had noticed a big change in her. She had lost weight and her spark. The Bible says that bad company corrupts good morals, and hanging around Trey had brought her down in every way. She had stopped attending the youth events, except on Sundays, when her parents made her come. When she was there, her attitude was one of disinterest. Sarah had even tried to drum up a conversation with her once or twice, but she would say something snide or just walk away when she saw her coming. Sarah felt her pain. She knew she was miserable. *I guess I'm just not the one to reach her,* Sarah complained to God one Sunday after being rudely ignored. *Oh, but you are, Sarah*, She heard God speak to her heart. *Okay God, I can't wait to see how you're going to do this. It's kind of hard to befriend someone who despises you and runs when they see you coming...but I know you have a plan and I trust You.*

Sarah didn't have to wait too long; the next day Jessica wasn't at school, which was surprising since they were voting for the Prom Court. Jessica's name was on the ballot, and

Sarah thought she would have wanted to be there to be a visual reminder for the people to vote for her. Prom was ironically on April 8–her due date. This would be one prom Sarah would have to miss. Jonathan was a shoe-in for the court, but had had his name taken off the ballot. No amount of coaxing would change his mind. He was going to be with Sarah, wherever that was.

Sarah wondered what kept Jessica from school. She hadn't looked sick at church the day before, but she didn't seem herself either. She seemed to be faking her life.

When Sarah went to Biology, Tyrone asked her what she was so "deep in thought" about.

She confided that she was just worried about Jessica, since she wasn't at school.

"Maybe you should call her. Just hearing your voice will surely bring healing to whatever ails her," Tyrone said in a smooth, sing-song voice.

Sarah just rolled her eyes and tried not to act amused.

"You really are concerned about the little..." He couldn't think of a word that Sarah would approve of, so he just trailed off to nothing.

"Yeah, I know it sounds crazy, but isn't God's love just that — crazy?" Sarah asked.

"It shoo is...so are you really thinking about calling her? Because if you are, this is one conversation I want to listen in on."

"No, silly, I'm not going to call her. I was just wondering what was wrong. She's just not been herself," Sarah answered.

"That could be good," Tyrone thought out loud.

Sarah couldn't help but smile. She knew what he meant. Then Tyrone got serious.

"You, little momma, do what my daddy preaches all the time — 'you love your enemies'. We'll see if it works, huh?"

"Yes, I guess we will."

The truth was, Sarah had seen Jessica and Trey several times lately, and they were always fighting. *Maybe they broke up. That would be a good thing.*

Jessica didn't come back to school till Wednesday. When she walked into first period, Sarah couldn't help but notice, she seemed shaken, lost, lethargic, and depressed. She avoided everyone and was very withdrawn. Sarah couldn't help herself. After class, she waited for Jessica outside the door. Sarah didn't know what she was going to say, she just knew she needed to say *something*.

"Jess, are you all right?" *Jess? Where did that endearment come from?* They were not on "nickname" terms but it just slipped out that way. Sarah was slightly embarrassed and it jarred Jessica.

She just looked at Sarah with a blank look and said, "No, there's nothing you can do. You—or anyone." Then she catatonically walked away. Sarah thought she had just talked to a robot. The shell was Jessica, but no one was home inside. Sarah hurt for her. What could have happened to change her so?

That afternoon, Sarah called Rachael.

"Maybe she's on drugs," Rachael guessed.

"I thought about that, but I don't think she's on drugs—she is hurting deeply. My guess is, it has to do with what she and Trey have been arguing about. Rachael, I know God wants to use me in her life, but I just feel so inadequate."

"Sarah, when you sat down at my lunch table that first day, I didn't know whether to stay or run. You carry a power and a presence that is overwhelming. It's the Holy Spirit and it got to me very quickly, and it will get to Jessica, too. The power of God is stronger than our will and Jessica's. Just wait and see."

On Thursday, Jonathan got a text from Jessica: "Can you give me Sarah's phone #?" Jonathan didn't know what to do, but felt like it had to be something important for her to ask him. Before he could think, he found himself texting Sarah's number back to her. Then he panicked—did he do the right thing? He quickly texted Sarah what had happened, so she would be prepared. The text to Sarah didn't go through right away, so she got the phone call first.

When Sarah's phone rang, she noticed a number she didn't recognize. She only got calls from three people: Jonathan, Rachael, and her dad. *Who could this be...*

"Hello?" Sarah answered.

The person on the other end didn't answer at first and Sarah almost hung up but she heard a sniffle then a muffled, "Sarah?" Sarah heard the fear in the voice.

"Yes, this is Sarah. Who is this?" Sarah realized the girl must be crying. She immediately thought of Brooke.

"Jessica," She managed to choke out.

Shock! Unbelief!

Sarah pulled it together, "Jessica, what's wrong? Are you in danger? Where are you?" Sarah was almost panicking. She knew it must be something serious for Jessica to be calling her crying.

"I need to talk to someone. Can I come over?" She asked humbly.

"Sure, come on."

"Thanks." Click.

Sarah almost fainted. She wondered if Jessica knew where she lived. She didn't have to wonder long because the doorbell rang. *She must have been sitting in my driveway when she called.*

Sarah ran—waddled, or whatever you do when you're eight months pregnant and trying to get somewhere fast—to get the door. She flung it open to find Jessica red-faced and snotty-nosed, standing there crying. She ran into Sarah's arms and cried for what seemed like forever. When Sarah didn't think she could hold her up any longer, Jessica pulled away and said. "Thanks for seeing me," like she was talking to a doctor.

"Come in!" Sarah motioned her to the closest couch.

Jessica sat down and started wailing.

Sarah was alarmed and wondering what could have happened that caused Jessica to be this upset. She moved beside her and handed her a Kleenex and grabbed one for herself. She rubbed her back in a light comforting motion not knowing what to do. She did the only thing she knew to do...she began to pray out loud.

"Father, I ask you to comfort my friend and bring her peace."

"Jessica," Sarah said in a low caring voice, "what happened? What is the matter?"

It took a few minutes for Jessica to be able to speak. When she did, she sobbed out, "I got pregnant."

Now Sarah understood why she came to her.

"Oh Jessica, I'm so sorry, but it's not the end of the world, I promise." Sarah consoled her.

"I got an abortion!" She whispered.

That was a kicker and something totally out of Sarah's expertise. All she knew about abortion was that it hurt, and messed girls up both physically and mentally.

"Oh Jessica. I'm so sorry."

"It was awful. What have I done? I hate myself. I killed my baby." She doubled over and just sobbed.

Sarah stepped over to the table and brought back the whole box of Kleenex.

Jessica took a few. Sarah didn't know what to say. She sat right next to her and put her arm around her. Jessica and Sarah both sat in silence crying. After what seemed like hours, Jessica started speaking.

"My mom made me go. She took me to the clinic. She said that there was no way I was going to walk around pregnant like 'that Sarah girl'."

Sarah was used to that, but it felt different coming from a mother. She decided to dismiss it.

"Now, I wish I had had the courage to do what you did. Trey was no help. He told me he didn't even know if it was his, so he wasn't taking any responsibility. He swore he always used a condom." Jessica blew her nose and wiped her eyes. "He's the only guy I've ever been with, but he wouldn't believe me."

"Maybe, he just doesn't *want* to believe you," Sarah added.

"Obviously not!" Jessica sobbed. "He hates me and so does God."

Sarah was praying hard. She felt totally out of her league counseling Jessica.

"Jessica, I've never had an abortion but I know that Jesus died for all sin and he has already died for your abortion. God doesn't hate you; He loves you and always has. Your abortion hasn't changed that one bit. You just need to ask his forgiveness and then forgive yourself. He does love you very much." Sarah was starting to cry herself. She couldn't imagine the pain Jessica was going through.

"I don't think I can. I'm a murderer!" she sobbed. "Isn't that one of the 'Big Ten'?"

"Yes, it's one of the Ten Commandments, but that's the point. Jesus' blood is stronger than the law. Mercy triumphs over judgment. God loves you and loves to give you mercy. That's the power of the cross!"

Sarah grabbed a Kleenex for herself and gave two to Jessica.

Jessica just listened like it was the first time she had ever heard about mercy and grace. Maybe she hadn't ever needed it like she did today.

Jessica blew her nose again and looked up at Sarah.

"Would you forgive me for being so mean to you?"

"I forgave you a long time ago. I always hoped one day, we'd be friends." That last statement was a stretch, but as she said it, she realized it was true.

"You're just so pretty. I knew Jonathan would like you—you're perfect for him. I was just so...jealous." Jessica admitted, still crying. "I've been so hateful to you, and you never fought back even though I know you wanted to. It made me just hate you more."

Sarah was dumbfounded by this whole confession.

"It's okay! Let's just forget the past and start over."

Jessica sat there for a few minutes trying to absorb everything and think about what came next.

"Let's pray about all this. Would that be okay?" Sarah asked.

"Yeah, that'd be good." Jessica answered.

Sarah started praying.

"Lord, I pray that You would comfort Jessica's hurting heart with Your love. Bathe her in Your comforting Holy Spirit. Bring Your healing to her heart and her body. Draw her close and comfort all her fears. Lord, you hold Jessica's future in Your hand and I pray that you would give Jessica hope. Assure her that there is nothing she can do to lose Your love. Thank you for allowing me to be a part of her life. In Jesus name, Amen"

Sarah was reminded of her words to Jessica in the hall about God being Jessica's healer. Now it made sense. Jessica needed healing. Sarah was witnessing Jessica rising from the grave.

"Thank you." Jessica sniffed.

"Jessica, there is one more thing I'd like to pray with you if you will. It's a prayer of repentance. I know that it is important to confess our sins. When we do, He promises to be faithful to forgive us."

Jessica broke down again. She was feeling the weight of her guilt. It took her a few minutes to get composed enough to answer.

"Yeah, I'd like that. I need forgiveness that's for sure."

"Do you want me to help you pray this?" Sarah asked.

"No, I think I can do this. Lord, please forgive me for walking away from You and choosing my own path. Forgive me for having sex with Trey even though I knew it was wrong. I'm sorry I broke your heart. And, especially forgive me for having this abortion. I'm so sorry." She broke down again and started wailing in pain. Sarah was crying too.

After they hugged again, Sarah got her some water. It was time for Jessica to get home for supper so she left after another hug.

As Jessica was walking out, she turned and said, "I'm sorry again for being so ugly to you. Thank you for letting me come over."

"You're forgiven, Jessica. I'm so glad you came over. I'll be praying for you. Call me if you need anything."

"Thanks," was all Jessica could get out. She turned and walked to her car. Sarah stood and watched as she backed out of the driveway.

As Sarah was closing the door she heard the familiar "ping" on her phone indicating she had a text. It was Jonathan, warning her that Jessica would be calling.

A little late! She was so overwhelmed at what God had done, she got on her knees and tearfully thanked God. "Thank you God, Your loving kindness is new every morning! Great is Your faithfulness!"

After supper, Jonathan called. He had to know if Jessica had called.

"Better than that! She came to my house!"

"What? Why? Did she hit you?" He was almost shouting.

"No!" Sarah said laughing. Then she told him Jessica was having a personal crisis and came to apologize for being so ugly to Sarah.

"I guess all my prayers were heard." Sarah finished. As much as Sarah would have loved to share with Jonathan about everything, she knew she couldn't tell him or anyone else, unless Jessica gave her permission. She had learned the importance of covering another's sins.

"I can't believe it! God has blown my mind this year. I have learned more from watching you walk out your relationship with the Lord than all the youth rallys and conferences I have ever attended! I feel what the disciples must have felt having gotten to walk with Jesus. You are an amazing girl, Sarah Levine."

"Thank you, Jonathan. I have been humbled by all of this, that's for sure. It has been an incredible journey. I guess this is what it means to 'walk in the spirit'." Sarah said.

35

Sarah could see the beginnings of spring out her window. The grass was beginning to turn green and the tulips that the former owner had planted in their yard were pushing up from the soil. Sarah could almost see them growing. Her life was beginning to blossom and soon she would be bringing new life from her own body. Her circumstances were definitely changing for the good. Promise and new life were all around her, filling her with hope and joy. *God, the firmament shows forth your handiwork...and it is so perfect!*

Sarah loved lying in her bedroom listening to the drone of her dad's voice as he talked to Nancy on his phone. Every few minutes, Sarah would hear Corbin cackle, as they relived their childhood, or their day, or whatever. He seemed so happy and light which made Sarah feel complete.

"So when am I going to get to meet Nancy and Tyler? I'm tired of just hearing about them," Sarah said one night at supper.

"Actually, you'll get to meet Nancy this weekend if your schedule isn't too full. Tyler has a track meet so he's staying in Austin with a friend," Corbin said teasingly.

"My schedule just got empty. When is she coming?" Sarah said, excited.

"She's driving in on Friday, and should be here by ten that night. She said she was free the whole day, Saturday, and was dying to spend some time with you...Now, what are we going to do?" Corbin asked nervously. He had no idea how they were going to entertain Nancy all day in Monroe with something she would enjoy.

"No problem. We'll start our morning at Shipley's Donut. That is one of Monroe's claims-to-fame." Sarah said in a professional tone.

"We could go out to Duck Dynasty and shop in their country store. Surely she needs a duck call," Corbin suggested sarcastically.

"I'm sure she would rather do something a little more cultural." Sarah laughed.

"You mean like a tour of Monroe? That will take all of fifteen minutes, especially if you hit the lights green," Corbin said.

They both laughed.

"Truthfully, Dad, there are *many* things to do in Monroe," Sarah said with confidence.

"We could go on a tour of Emie Lou Beidenharn's house. I heard the gardens are a great place to take pictures. They also have a Coca-Cola machine where you can get a five-cent Coke."

"This date is getting cheaper by the minute!" Corbin said.

"Right..."

"Now, tell me again who Emie Lou was?" Corbin asked.

"She was an eccentric opera singer whose father was one of the men who first bottled Coca-Cola. Needless to say, the Beidenharns were famous and rich," Sarah informed him.

"Those are good ideas...she might really enjoy all those things. What else does your tour include?" Corbin teased.

"Well, for an add-on, which will be extra, we could have Johnny's Pizza for lunch, unless she's watching her figure

Sarah's Story

and then we could have salad at the Holiday Inn." She and her father both gave the salad a thumbs-down.

"Then, after lunch, we could cross the river and go to Antique Alley. She'll love that!"

"And, I'll *endure* it." Shopping was not one of Corbin's fortes.

"Yes, you will...and with a smile—and no complaints," Sarah said in her little mother voice.

"Yes, ma'am. Anything else?" Corbin said, choking back a snicker.

"Yes, just two more things. After a leisurely afternoon of shopping, let's eat crawfish at Cormier's for supper."

"That sounds like a perfect Louisiana day! And, how much do I owe you for planning this scrumptious itinerary?" Corbin said, trying to act very 'French'. Then remembering..."What is your second thing?"

"Would it be okay if Jonathan joined us for crawfish?"

"Sure, she'd love to meet Jonathan—he's practically family, and by then I'm going to probably want some male company."

"Thanks, Daddy!" Sarah said, hugging him and giving him a kiss. "You're the greatest!"

"No, you're the greatest!" Corbin responded.

"Does Nancy know I'm pregnant?" Sarah asked, figuring he had told her.

"Of course! She knows all about you and thinks you're a hero to the Christian faith."

Sarah was relieved. She could hardly wait until the weekend. *What a miracle that Nancy's sister would end up in West Monroe.*

When she told Jonathan, he was glad to be included.

The rest of the week dragged by for Sarah. She couldn't wait to meet Nancy and get to spend some time with her.

The kids at school didn't know what to think about her and Jessica's new friendship. Tyrone was beside himself.

"Did my eyes deceive me or was that Jessica I saw you talking to before school?" He could tell by their body language that it was not a hostile meeting.

"Your eyes were witnessing a downright miracle!" Sarah beamed.

"A miracle, right here on our campus! Wait till my dad hears about this. You are going to be the subject of his sermon next week—you just wait and see! You might want to jump camps and come over to the Pentecostal church and hear this!"

Sarah couldn't help but laugh.

"I know. I can hardly believe it myself. Jessica just needed some redeeming love, and that is what God gave her."

Tyrone begged to know what changed everything, so Sarah told him that they just had a girl heart-to-heart talk and everything got put together. He knew there was more to it than that, but since Sarah wasn't sharing, he decided he better not push. He knew how girls could love each other one day, and hate each other the next, so he just chalked it up to 'females'.

"Well, all I can say is, I would have never believed it if I hadn't have seen it with my own eyes! Way to go!"

On Thursday, she received a letter in the mail. She saw Ms. Hamm's return address and started trembling with excitement. She ran inside and tore the envelope open.

Dear Sarah,

Thank you for your sweet letter. I am so glad to get to have an opportunity to tell you how encouraging your words were that day you walked in on me crying. God heard your prayers, and I told my parents that night. They

Sarah's Story

were disappointed, but now that they've recovered, they have been extremely supportive. I wanted to be able to finish the school year, or at least come back and say goodbye, but I decided to let you retain the pregnancy spotlight! Thank you for keeping our secret. I so admire your courage and strength. I know I told you that before, but when I think I can't go on, or I start punishing myself because of what I did, I think of you and the day that you played Hester with such dignity and grace.

God bless you. You're my inspiration!

Ms. Hamm

Sarah read the last of the letter through her tears. Thank you Lord! Please bless Ms. Hamm and her baby.

When Saturday finally arrived, it came with the most perfect weather. Instead of the humid Louisiana air, a cool front had come in. *Great hair day!* The sun was going to be shining all day but the temperature was supposed to be around sixty-five to seventy degrees. Sarah knew the weather was a special gift from God. She was filled with anticipation. She didn't get too much sleep the night before and neither did Corbin. She told her dad she felt like she was going on her first date. He told her he felt the same way, too.

They were to be at Susan and Rick's house at eight that morning, for an early start. Susan and Rick lived in a subdivision out in the hills of West Monroe. The ride over there was a tour in itself. The houses were spaced apart and every one of them different. They all seemed to have manicured lawns with beautiful flower gardens. Susan's was no different. She was a great gardener, so her pansies were beautiful. Her house looked like a picture postcard. Nancy had helped with the inside, so it was equally perfect. Nancy opened the door with a warm greeting. Nancy hugged her first, which Sarah took note of. Then she hugged Corbin. Sarah and Nancy were both so glad to finally meet. They went in for a minute to say "hi" to Susan and Rick, but Susan shooed them off so they could enjoy their day.

On the drive to Shipley's Donuts, Nancy asked Sarah about her baby and school and Jonathan and Rachael. Corbin had told her everything and she had remembered it well. Sarah felt included and very grateful. They were at Shipley's in no time. Shipley's was founded over seventy-six years ago and the decor didn't appear to have been touched since it was first opened. The green vinyl booths were slit with wear and the linoleum on the tables was worn down to the wood in places. Even the donuts were the original recipe, which was a good thing. It was like walking into your grandma's kitchen. The aroma was enough to take one back to a magical time when all was well with the world. Shipley's offered filled, glazed, or cake donuts so they ordered one of each and had a taste-eating contest. They all agreed that while they were all good, the glazed was their favorite. They didn't want to eat too much because the day was going to be full of food, so they all had a total of one donut each. Then it was on to Emi Lou Biedenharn's. Her museum was about one mile from Shipley's, down Riverside. Sarah pointed out the plantation houses to Nancy along the way. Nancy loved the charm and originality of each house.

"We certainly don't have this in Austin." Nancy commented.

"Look, that house has a servants quarters built on to the house." Sarah said pointing to a beautiful plantation with a smaller house next to it.

"I would love to know the story behind these houses." Corbin commented.

"Well, we are about to hear the story behind one of them." Sarah said proudly.

"Sarah, this was such a great idea. I would not have known Monroe had such a rich past." Nancy praised her.

"Yeah, me neither." Corbin said, trying to share their enthusiasm.

As they walked up the steps of Emi Lou's Museum, Corbin commented, "This house looks more like the First National Bank."

"Yeah, they probably owned that too. I think the Biedenharns owned most of the town at the time."

The tour was fascinating. Nancy and Sarah loved to see Emi Lou's bedroom and her old clothes.

"Look at how small the beds were. These were some really short people." Sarah observed.

"With some really small feet." Nancy added looking at the shoes she wore. "I wish my feet were this small and petite. Shoes look better if they're smaller."

"Really, I always wanted bigger feet." Corbin said.

"Oh, Daddy, that's because you're a man."

"Oh, is that what I am. Thanks. I need to hear that every now and then." He said teasingly.

Nancy and Sarah laughed.

"Here is the five cent Coke machine. We have to get one for novelty's sake."

"Okay, the Cokes are on me." Corbin said.

Nancy and Sarah just looked at each other and shook their heads.

In the backyard was a beautiful garden with a rounded platform attached to the house. The tour guide explained that many brides chose to have their engagement picture taken there.

"Daddy, you and Nancy climb up there and let me take your picture." Corbin and Nancy both sheepishly scaled the steps and posed on the stoop while she took the picture. Then she had the tour guide to take one of all three of them.

After being there for two hours, Sarah turned to Nancy and her dad and said, "I think I've had enough culture for one day. Is it time for lunch?"

Corbin and Nancy laughed. "Not exactly, so let's go over to the park and sit in the shade."

That was an excellent idea. They found a nice oak tree with a bench under it where the breeze was blowing and sat down.

"She was a very extraordinary woman." Nancy was saying of Emi Lou.

"It made me tired just thinking about all her accomplishments. She definitely left a legacy behind." Corbin agreed.

"Makes me wonder what kind of legacy I will leave behind." Sarah mused out loud.

"I know this. It's going to be something big." Corbin said with confidence.

"Thanks, Daddy." Corbin had always been one of Sarah's most loyal fans even if he was her father. He knew Sarah would accomplish great things for the kingdom. She already was.

Finally, it was time for lunch. Sarah's one donut was long gone. She was glad they only had to drive a half mile to the pizza place. Nancy commented on how compact everything was. It was obvious Johnny's was another family business by the thirty-year old tables and benches.

"You can't judge this place by its interior decorator. The pizza is the best in town. Truthfully, it's probably the best I've ever had." Sarah told Nancy as they were walking in.

Nancy looked around and agreed Johnny needed to change decorators for sure.

Sarah's Story

Corbin turned to the two and asked, "So, what are you two beautiful ladies going to have?"

Sarah answered first. "Let's do a safe one and a dare one!"

"What?" Nancy and Corbin asked at the same time.

"Well, since Johnny's has such off-the-wall pizzas, let's order one that is predictable and we know we will all like, like pepperoni. Then let's order something that we would never order and try it for fun. Like alligator pizza."

"That sounds like an interesting idea. So.... ladies, what will it be? Alligator, Crab?"

They looked over the menu that hung above the check out desk. "I think we should see what armadillo pizza tastes like." Nancy suggested.

"It's going to be hard to eat something you usually see dead on the side of the road." Corbin joked.

Sarah was not so sure she was going to be able to handle it herself, but love makes you do strange things, so Corbin and Sarah agreed to try it.

By the time it was their turn to order, they had changed it to crabmeat pizza. At least you could order crab at a restaurant. Sarah had never seen roadkill on a menu before.

"This is definitely a cheat day today," Nancy said.

"Yeah, I don't usually eat this way either. I hope Samuel is enjoying this," Sarah said.

"I'm going to probably pay for this tonight," Corbin added.

They enjoyed their lunch. Sarah couldn't get over how easy it was to be with Nancy. It was like she had always been a part of the family. Even though she would rather it be her mom, it was so good to see her dad happy and laughing again. She loved hearing their stories of growing up together... and they had plenty. She learned that her dad was quite the jokester as a kid. After lunch, it was on to Antique Alley.

Antique Alley was a real treat for the girls. It was a street lined with charming boutiques and interesting shops. Corbin had secretly texted Jonathan to come rescue him, so Jonathan

Sarah's Story

just "showed up" and sat with Corbin on the bench, where they played games on their phones together and watched people. Sarah and Nancy didn't mind because it gave them time to spend together. Sarah found some "after baby" clothes and Nancy found some designer jeans. Sarah saw the perfect dress for prom.... only she wouldn't be going to prom this year. It made her sad for a few minutes. They all went to the costume shop and tried on different masks and cut up. By the end of the day, Sarah and Nancy felt like they had shopped till they were about to drop. Supper would be a much needed rest for their feet.

On the way, Jonathan filled Nancy in on their next stop.

"Cormier's is a restaurant where you sit outside on picnic tables. They give each person the top to a cardboard box full of crawfish, corn on the cob and potatoes, all heavily seasoned with Tony Chachere's. By the end of the meal, your lips will be on fire. Who else has ever been to Cormier's?" Jonathan asked looking around the car. No one raised their hands.

"Ya'll have never eaten at Cormiers?" Jonathan asked in total unbelief.

"Nope." Sarah answered for all of them.

"Well, you're in for a treat. Please tell me ya'll know how to eat crawfish?"

Silence.

"Unbelievable. Ya'll haven't lived yet. Just wait. I am going to school ya'll in the art of eating crawfish." Jonathan said, proudly.

"Why do you think we invited you to come?" teased Sarah.

"I should have let ya'll come alone and make a fool of yourselves." Jonathan teased back.

They got in line and got their box of food and went to the picnic tables. Everyone looked at Jonathan for their lesson. Corbin waved his hand for Jonathan to begin.

"First, you break off the head like this." He broke off his head and waited for them to follow.

"Then you suck the head."

"Yuck!"

"Gross!"

"I don't think I can do that." They all had their comments.

"Yes, you can. Is steak the only thing ya'll know how to eat?" Jonathan teased, patiently waiting for them to follow his instructions. They did reluctantly.

"At least we don't have to suck the cow's head," Nancy added.

They all laughed.

"Now, wasn't that delish?" Jonathan said, moving quickly to the next command in case they didn't like it. "Then you break off the tail," Jonathan demonstrated. "Without any comments," He added.

"That's no fun," Sarah said with a smile.

"Then you open up the scales and take out the meat," Jonathan concluded.

"And, what do you do with this tiny morsel of food?" Corbin asked sarcastically.

"You eat it. Eating crawfish is about the experience." He ate his bite and said, "Yum! And that, my folks, is the Louisiana way to eat a crawfish!" He stood up and took a bow.

"Ouch!" screamed Nancy as she rubbed her eyes.

"Oh, I forgot to tell you, sometimes they splatter, so you have to watch it. Sorry," Jonathan said, shrugging his shoulders as if to say "sometimes you just have to take one for the team".

"Well, now I know why they bring you a mound of crawfish. Each crawfish represents two bites!" Corbin teased.

Jonathan turned to Sarah and said, "Are your children always this picky?"

"Yes, they are!" Sarah said laughing.

"But, thank you Jonathan for your demonstration. That was just downright cultural. Thank goodness pregnant women aren't supposed to eat much crawfish...I think I'll stick to the veggies." Sarah said in her most southern belle drawl.

"You're mighty welcome, Miss Sarah," Jonathan answered back in his southern gentleman drawl.

They ate and visited underneath the stars till ten. It was the ending of a perfect day!

36

The next day at church, Sarah wanted to be sure to reach out to Jessica. She didn't want the devil to have a chance to steal what God had done in their relationship. When Jessica walked in, Sarah walked straight over and hugged her and asked how she was doing. She seemed relieved and told her she was doing better. Jonathan came up and spoke friendly with her too. Sarah invited Jessica to sit with her and Jonathan in church. Whether she wanted to or not, she said yes. Sarah wondered what Jessica's friends thought about seeing this new development. Jessica seemed so broken and pathetic, Sarah doubted if she cared. For the first time, Jessica needed someone, and right now it was Sarah. Jessica couldn't talk to her friends about the abortion. Jessica and her friends had talked about girls who got abortions, never dreaming that one day it would be one of them. Sarah could sense that Jessica needed a lot of care and found herself asking her to spend the night with her that next Friday. To her surprise, Jessica gladly took her up on it. She said she would be there right after her dance class.

Sarah just laughed to herself. *God, you are amazing!*

When she told Rachael everything, she was so proud of Sarah.

"I have to admit, I'm a little jealous." Rachael teased.

"Rachael, no one will ever take your place. You are my BFF! You are my David and I am your Jonathan." They had often teased about that.

"I know you're right. I'll be praying for you. This is so much fun...I never knew life could be so fun with God."

Sarah was a little apprehensive about what she and Jessica would talk about when she arrived to spend the night. She had prepared some questions to get her talking about herself. Everyone loves to talk about themselves, and Sarah wanted to get to know her.

Jessica arrived around 5:30.

"So how was your dance lessons?" Sarah started as she was escorting Jessica to her room.

"It was okay. My teacher expects me to be able to do everything perfect. She's just like my mom. My mom wants me to be a famous dancer, a Dallas Cowboy cheerleader, a straight 'A' student, and a perfect Christian which is stressful! Truth is, I'm not good enough at any of those things to be famous. I just want to enjoy my life...and not always be competing. Know what I mean?" Jessica confided.

"Yeah, I would hate to be famous. They have no privacy and are usually misunderstood." Sarah said, thinking about what Jessica had just said. Now she understood why Jessica was like she was.

"It *would* be nice to be rich—but then you already know about that don't you?" Jessica said matter-of-factly.

Sarah didn't know how to respond to that so she just let it pass.

By that time they had reached Sarah's room.

"Wow! What a cool room! Did you have one of those interior decorators do it?"

Sarah smiled, "No, I did it myself. Glad you like it!"

"How did you paint these walls like this? I love the stripes!"

Sarah didn't want to tell her that Jonathan had helped her, so she just explained the procedure.

"Anyone can do it," she concluded.

"Well, I couldn't. I don't have the patience," Jessica confessed.

Sarah took Jessica around her room answering her questions about how she made this, or where she bought that. After a while, they heard her dad shout up, "Supper's here."

They went downstairs.

"I hope you like Pepperoni or Hamburger," Sarah said as they descended the stairs. She was getting rather large and she was out of breath by the time she reached the bottom. Jessica noticed.

"I like both. It must be hard to carry around a baby all the time." A sadness passed over her face when she said it.

Sarah understood what she must be thinking. Jessica could be pregnant now, too. Sarah hoped they would be able to talk about it later.

"It is getting harder and harder, that's for sure."

"Well, hello, Jessica! We're so glad you could come and enjoy our Friday night ritual with us." Corbin welcomed.

"He's right. We have pizza just about every Friday night."

"We do too. I think just about everyone in Monroe does."

They all laughed and agreed.

They ate at the kitchen table, which was a habit Kathy had started at Sarah's birth. She didn't want her family eating in front of the TV and not having conversation.

Corbin kept them entertained with funny antics about his childhood. Reuniting with Nancy had brought back so many memories he had forgotten. She had also brought joy back to Corbin.

After supper, she and Jessica went into the sunroom to see if there was a good movie on.

"Do you and your dad always talk like that?" Jessica asked.
"Like what?"

"Like y'all actually *like* each other and enjoy being together."

"Yeah, we do...we always have. It was easier when my mom was alive. We had to work on it after she left, but now it's easy."

"I wish I had that with my parents. My mom is always busy with her own social life and my dad works all the time. The only time we eat together is Sunday at Ryan's after church—but I don't call that 'family time.' Everyone's on their cell phones and we hardly talk except when my mom tells my brother not to eat too much, and my little sister to sit up straight and *to* eat!"

"Maybe you could suggest a 'kitchen table night' where everyone has to eat at home," Sarah offered, feeling sorry for Jessica.

"I'm sure that would go over great!" Jessica said sarcastically.

They resumed looking through the TV menu for a movie. When they couldn't find anything worth watching they gave up, went up to Sarah's room, got on their p.j.s and perched on Sarah's bed.

"Jess, how are you feeling about everything?" Sarah started.

"You mean the abortion and all...Well, I don't miss Trey that's for sure! He was a real jerk and treated me like dirt. I don't know why it took me so long to figure that out! But I feel...empty about the abortion. It's like I aborted God's plan and changed history. I have nightmares about it. Last night I dreamed that someone was in my bedroom window and when I went to shut it so he couldn't get in, he grabbed my hands and tried to pull me out of the window. I screamed 'help' over and over until my parents finally came in and woke me up. I felt this fear that I've never felt before. It was really scary!"

Sarah grabbed her Bible and turned to 2 Timothy 1:7 and read aloud, "Listen to this: 'God has not given us a spirit of fear, but of power, love and a sound mind.' It sounds like a spirit of fear is trying to get in and steal your peace and your joy."

"So you think my dream means something?" Jessica sounded amazed.

"Yes, God speaks to me through my dreams all the time. He spoke to many people in the Bible that way. About one third of the Bible is about dreams," Sarah explained.

"So you think that those hands were a spirit trying to pull me out of my house? Jessica asked.

"Yeah, I think they were just that. In a dream, your house is you and your place of safety and security. The devil is the thief who comes to kill and steal from us."

"So...what do I do? When we prayed last week I felt so much better, but slowly I felt myself fall back into a pit and I just don't seem to be able to get out," Jessica said with tears in her eyes.

Sarah reached for her Bible again and turned to Ephesians 6:10-18 and read about the armor of God. She would read a verse then stop, and they would discuss it and what each piece represented. When they got to the part about the "sword of the spirit, which is the Word of God", Sarah asked Jessica if she read her Bible regularly.

"No. I don't read it, because I never know where to start, or understand what I read. I could never pick it up, and find something like you just did. How do you do that?"

"Well, I guess it's because my Mom used to read the Bible to me, every night. She taught me how to find 'help' scripture like the one I just read to you. The more you read the Bible, the more you understand it."

"Yeah, I've heard that scripture about the armour all my life, only I've never dissected and understood it like I do today. So do you read your Bible every day?"

"Yes! I can't think of not reading it. Sometimes I read it several times a day. When I'm sad and need encouragement,

I turn to the Psalms and just start reading until something jumps out at me. If I need wisdom, I read Proverbs 1, 2, or 3 and pray for wisdom. A couple of years ago my parents gave me a plan to read through the Bible in a year and I've been doing it ever since."

"You're kidding! You read through the *whole* Bible every year! I didn't know anyone but preachers did that!"

Sarah chuckled, which made Jessica smile.

"Well, one thing's for sure, I'm no preacher!" Sarah laughed, then continued, "It was hard the first year, and it's still hard in some parts like Leviticus, but now I even like them. The Holy Spirit's job is to help us understand the Bible. All we have to do is ask him."

"I guess you can't understand something you don't read," Jessica said thoughtfully.

"No, I guess not." Sarah said with a smile. Jessica smiled back.

"Let's pray about all this." Sarah said.

"Okay!" said Jessica excitedly, then her face got serious. "Could we pray about something else? It's going to sound silly and maybe we shouldn't bother God about it, but since I broke up with Trey, I don't have a date to the prom. I'm so embarrassed, and all the good guys already have dates."

"God would love for you to bother him with that—if it's important to you, it's important to him."

Sarah was sitting cross-legged in front of Jessica, so she took her hands and prayed, "Lord, thank you for bringing Jessica into my life to be my friend. We know that you didn't give Jessica the spirit of fear, but of power, love and a sound mind so we bind and cast out this spirit of fear, and in its place we put the spirit of God's power, God's love, and His mind. Help Jessica overcome her hesitancy to read the Bible. And Holy Spirit, I ask you to speak to Jessica every time she opens Your Word. I pray that Your peace and Your joy will be Jessica's strength. Use everything Jessica has gone through for your glory. And Lord, would You send Jessica a good date for Prom. In Jesus name, amen." Sarah almost ended it with, "and, help me to love Jessica", but stopped herself, just in time.

"Thanks, that was a perfect prayer. No more stealing from me, you devil!" Jessica said with boldness.

"That's the way to speak to the devil—with authority! The Bible says: 'greater is he that is in you, than he who is in the world,'" Sarah encouraged.

"Amen!" Jessica said with great enthusiasm.

They both got tickled and started laughing. They laughed so hard Sarah rolled right off the bed. Then they really cracked up.

They stayed up talking about school and girl stuff. Jessica never asked her about how she got pregnant and Sarah was thankful.

They both knew they had to get up early, so at eleven o'clock, when Sarah couldn't stop yawning, Jessica let her go to sleep. They were both tired. Sarah played her tape of Hannah's scriptures and Jessica slept like a baby.

The next morning they ate breakfast and went to Amber Ross's house to make decorations for prom. Everyone was noticeably uncomfortable when Sarah walked in with Jessica—now who were they going to talk about? And,...what was Jessica doing befriending the enemy? They tried—too hard—to be cordial to Sarah.

Sarah was so used to people being uncomfortable around her, that it didn't matter that much. She did her best just to be herself.

Listening to her friend's conversations made Jessica realize how catty she used to be. Sarah was determined to have something good come out of the situation. It helped when Sarah was able to give them some good ideas about things they could make. She had done so much decorating with her mom, who had the gift of hospitality. They were always decorating for parties. After a while, they were all working on tissue paper flowers and leaves and stems, etc. They laughed and carried on like they were old friends. They even laughed at Sarah's pregnant jokes. She only had four more weeks to go and her whole stomach moved when Samuel decided to move. The girls watched in rapt amazement watching Sarah's stomach roll. They all wanted to feel the baby move. Many of them had never seen or felt that before, especially on someone their age. It gave them a totally different perspective.

Someone asked Sarah if she was going to the prom. The room got strangely quiet waiting her answer.

"I'll be dancing in the delivery room. Prom is on my due date." That seemed to sober them up.

"So ya'll will have to do a dance for me," she said trying to lighten the moment. It worked because then they all tried to come up with a "pregnant dance". It was hilarious.

Sarah had to leave at noon because she and Jonathan had planned to go see Rachael and Luke for an afternoon movie in Ruston. She excused herself to leave. Jessica walked Sarah to the door and thanked her for having her spend the night.

37

Sarah's new English teacher was an older lady named Ms. Talbert. She was a well-seasoned teacher who was strong in discipline, which Sarah liked. She gave them the assignment of writing a paper on someone in their life who had inspired them. They were asked if anyone wanted to voluntarily read theirs aloud. One of the girls in her class, that Sarah barely knew, raised her hand to read her paper out loud. She had written about Sarah! She wrote about the day that Sarah had to stand in front of the class and play the part of Hester, and how that had inspired her to be brave in the face of ridicule and hard times. She had used that so many times in her fights with insecurity and weakness. When she finished, the whole class clapped. Sarah was touched to tears, as many of the girls were. She had no idea people were positively affected by that. *God thank you for letting me see the fruit of that horrible experience.*

The blanket she had been working on with Lucille was finally finished and Sarah couldn't wait to give it to Hannah.

Lucille told Sarah that her husband, Harry, had been a handsome Puerto Rican. She used to lovingly call him her Ricky Ricardo and he called her his Lucille Ball. They looked forward to watching the 'I Love Lucy' episodes every week.

Sarah's Story

Sarah had found out that the theater at the mall was showing a day of 'I Love Lucy' reruns. With permission, she checked Lucille out for an afternoon at the movies.

"I feel like I'm riding off in the 'get-away car'." Lucille said once they got in Sarah's car.

"And what experience have you had with 'get-away cars'? Is there something I should know?"

"My record is clear... at least, up until now. I'm not sure what you have planned for today." They both laughed.

"My plan is to take you back sixty years and give you an afternoon of fun and laughter. You know what the Bible says about laughter."

"It doeth good like a medicine." Lucille finished.

"Yes, it doeth!" Sarah giggled.

They got to the mall at 9:30 to get their tickets and buy drinks and popcorn. They sat in their seats and visited until it started. Lucille could only stay till two, but they loved every episode, especially the one about the chocolate factory. They laughed and cried. Two o'clock came too soon. As Sarah walked Lucille to her room, Lucille beamed,

"This was the most fun that I've had in years. Thank you so much, Sarah."

"The pleasure was all mine." Sarah answered truthfully.

Jessica and some of the girls in the youth group had gotten together and planned a baby shower for Sarah and Samuel. Even though they knew Sarah wouldn't be keeping Samuel, they wanted to welcome him into the world. Jessica's mom had a change of heart about Sarah and readily agreed to help. They reserved the church fellowship hall for the Saturday before her due date. Hannah and Drew were coming to Monroe so Sarah asked if it would be okay to invite Hannah to the shower also, since she would be Samuel's mother. Everyone loved the idea since they wanted to meet her also. The girls asked for a list of what Samuel would need since

Sarah's Story

Hannah was limited with how much stuff she could take on the plane. Sarah had Hannah give her a wish list and asked everyone to please stick to the list.

At the party, Sarah insisted that Hannah open every other gift. They played games and ate Southern hors d'oeuvres. It was a blessing to everyone who came and Hannah got everything on her list! Before it was time to go, the girls surprised Sarah with a special gift. It was a necklace with an "S" on it for "Samuel". Sarah was surprised and touched.

When Sarah had a moment alone with Jessica, she asked her if she had a date for prom yet. She told her, no, but she was still believing God for one. Jessica was trying so hard to have faith, but Sarah could tell she was struggling.

"I know it's going to be great. Do you have your dress yet?" Sarah asked her.

"Yes, I've had my dress forever," Jessica answered.

"Good! God's going to do amazing things for you...you just wait and see."

"Okay, Sarah, I'm standing on your faith."

"That's okay. I have enough for both of us." She did. Sarah had seen God do too many things to doubt Him now.

D-day was quickly approaching. Sarah had one week to go. School had become physically hard. Walking up and down the stairs was a workout. She learned to take them slowly. She insisted on going to school until the baby came. Spring break started the next week, so she would have a week off to recuperate. It never entered Sarah's mind that she might be late. She knew God, and his timing was perfect. She also knew, for Hannah and Drew, the baby had to come on its due date. It never dawned on her that he might come early since her doctor kept telling her he would be late.

That week, at school, everything was about the prom. Everyone was so pepped up that the teachers didn't plan to teach any new concepts. They knew it would be futile.

Jessica had changed so much that everyone noticed. She became more outgoing. Compassion replaced conceit. Tyrone couldn't get over it.

Sarah smiled. *God, thank you again for the power of a changed heart. Now about that prom date for Jessica...thank you for the perfect guy.*

38

On Wednesday, the fifth, Sarah woke up at three in the morning to false labor pains. The doctor had informed her that theses were called Braxton hicks and that many women had them off and on during their pregnancy. She had them before and knew what they were. They stayed with her while she was preparing for school, and were still going strong during first period. Sarah was sitting in Pre-Cal when suddenly she felt her chair get wet. At first she thought she had peed in her pants, then she realized what had happened. Her water had broken! Her baby was coming...now! Today! Her face must have showed her surprise, because Jessica was over at her desk in an instant. Ms. Tanner was demonstrating a problem on the board and didn't know what was happening till she noticed the water on the floor.

"Oh my, we need to get you to the office! Jessica, take Sarah to the office and tell them to send the custodian back with a mop."

"Yes, Ms. Tanner," Jessica said as she helped Sarah get up and get her stuff together. Sarah already had her phone out and was calling her dad. She didn't care if she did get in trouble for using her phone—this was an emergency. She also texted Rachael: DD, which was their code for "D-day".

Corbin was like a bumbling first-time father. He sped all the way to the school and got there by the time Sarah got checked out. Jessica had called her mom and asked if she could check out, too. Her mom agreed, so she rode with them to the hospital. Before they left, Jessica sweet-talked the girl working at the desk to send Jonathan a note telling him what was going on. When she found out it was for Jonathan, she was good. Who wouldn't want to take Jonathan a note?

So off to the hospital they went. Of all the scenarios Sarah had imagined, this was not one of them. She figured she would have it on Saturday, where no one would know till it was over. The last thing she wanted to happen was to lose her water in class! *God you seem to love embarrassing me! You seem bent on letting everyone in on my life! So much for Dr. Abel thinking I was coming late.*

On the way to the hospital, she texted Hannah and Lucille. She wanted Lucille to be praying for her and Hannah to be with her. Hannah and Drew were coming into the delivery room with her, even though Dr. Abel didn't much like it. Since Sarah was one of his favorites, he said he would bend a few of his cardinal rules. He let Sarah know that if anything unusual happened he was throwing everyone out. *The doctor! I haven't even told him I'm coming!* She called his office and told them that she was in labor. They assured her they would be praying for her and that they would tell Dr. Abel.

Hannah and Drew arrived and were as nervous as Sarah. The waiting room was full of the people who supported her... all excited and noisy. Corbin was relieved to have them there with him. They helped Sarah get admitted and followed her to her room. Sarah was having contractions three minutes apart. This baby was coming soon. They hooked her up to a monitor and told her the doctor would be there soon. Since his office was close to the hospital, he was there in a few minutes. When Dr. Abel arrived and examined her, he got a very surprised look on his face.

Sarah's Story

"This baby is coming...quickly!" He said excitedly.

Jonathan walked into the room right as Dr. Abel was asking everyone to leave. Sarah reminded the doctor that Hannah and Drew were staying. Drew remained by the door to respect Sarah's privacy. Hannah stood by Sarah and held her hand.

Sarah's contractions were on top of each other and hard. She had opted to go natural because she read it was best for the baby. They watched the contractions on the monitor and were counting their length. Dr. Abel came in quickly and examined her one more time.

"You weren't kidding when you said you were in labor. You've been in labor for a while." Dr. Abel said right before he told her she could push.

Sarah only had to push three times before the doctor said, "One more push and the head will be out."

She could see Hannah's face light up as she felt Samuel come into the world. It was priceless. She heard Samuel cry and she started crying herself.

The nurse asked Sarah if she wanted to hold him. Even though Sarah wanted to, she had already decided that Hannah needed to be the first one to hold Samuel.

"No, give him to his mother," and pointed to Hannah. Hannah was crying as she took Samuel and took him over to where Drew was standing. Hannah returned and took Sarah's hand, looked into her eyes and said,

"Sarah, I don't know how to express how thankful we are for you. You have given us the greatest gift and paid an incredible sacrifice. We will always love you and Samuel will always know how brave you are.

Sarah felt so blessed to be used to bring them such joy. The moment Samuel left her body, she felt unattached to him, like he wasn't her baby. It was amazing. God had really just used her body to bring them a baby. She was tremendously happy for them. They held him up for her to see that he was a beautiful baby. She told them he looked like them. They seemed appreciative. They kept thanking Sarah over and over.

Sarah was tired and the nurse could tell and asked everyone to leave so she could get some rest. She was given something for pain and slept for five hours. They had given her a pill for her milk to dry up, so she didn't have to worry about waking up to nurse Samuel. As far as she was concerned, this was Hannah's baby and Hannah was now in charge.

Sarah gave Hannah the blanket she had knitted for Samuel, and Hannah wrapped him in it.

There was a constant flow of visitors coming in and out of Sarah's room. Nancy and her son Tyler had come to visit so Sarah finally got to meet Tyler. He was handsome and funny. He and Jonathan sat and talked sports for an hour. Rachael stayed the morning, then had to get home to watch Joey. Luke had to work but sent Sarah a homemade card. He had written her a hilarious poem. Luke was a real song writer. He promised in the note to sing the poem to her when he saw her next. Sarah laughed till she cried. Christy, Melissa, Emma and Kate all came together and stayed a while and Jessica came that afternoon. When Jessica came in she seemed really happy. They were finally alone for enough time for Jessica to tell her the exciting news.

"You'll never believe this....Yes, you will.... I have a date to the prom!" Jessica almost shouted.

"That's awesome! Who is it?" Sarah asked just as excited.

"I just met him....he's not from here." Jessica was interrupted as the door opened and in walked Tyrone.

"Hey little momma!" Tyrone boomed. He was carrying some flowers he had picked from his gramma's garden.

"Tyrone! You're so sweet to come see me."

"I had to. After all I went through with you, I feel like I've been pregnant these nine months. I had to come see what we had."

"You're right." Sarah laughed, "I couldn't have done it without you. Have you met Jessica?" Sarah said with a knowing smile.

"Hey Jessica, nice to meet you." Tyrone said, trying to act like he had never discussed her everyday in Biology. Then, holding out his flowers to Sarah he said, "My gramma wanted me to give you these. She told me to tell you, she's proud of you." Tyrone turned to Jessica and said, "My gramma thinks she's Sarah's gramma, too." Jessica took them and set them on the shelf beside her bed.

"Tyrone! That is so sweet of her. Tell her I love them. They're beautiful and I think it's me who adopted her! Did you see Samuel?"

"Yeah! He's going to be a football player for sure. He was lying there throwing a pass with his arms." Sarah and Jessica both laughed.

Before Tyrone left, Corbin, Nancy and Tyler came back in.

"Sarah, I want you to meet my date to prom!" Jessica said gesturing at Tyler. Sarah just shook her head in amazement. Tyler was grinning ear to ear. God had definitely answered their prayer!

39

All of Samuel's vital signs were strong and good. Sarah was doing so well that they told her she could go home the next day! She was ecstatic! Hannah would stay at the hospitol with Samuel. He was now their son. Sarah did finally hold Samuel right before they left the hospital.

Nancy stayed with Sarah during the day while Corbin was at work. They had some really good talks and were able to establish a close bond.

"So, Sarah, since you're doing so well, what about going to the prom?" Nancy asked her on Friday.

"I don't even have a dress!" she said.

"Remember that beautiful vintage dress we saw at Antique Alley? The one you said would be what you would wear if you were going?"

"Yeah, I remember. I'm sure it's gone by now," Sarah said.

"Well, I called about it a little while ago and it's still there so I asked them to hold it." Nancy said excitedly.

"Really, I wonder if Jonathan wants to go?" Sarah said with hope rising in her heart.

Beep!

Sarah had a text. It was from Jonathan. It said: *I was wondering if you would feel like going with me to the prom. We can leave when you get tired.*

"Well, I guess I have my answer. Call and tell them we want the dress." She showed Nancy the text. They both cackled. "God's timing is impeccable!"

Sarah texted back: *I would love to!*

The phone rang. It was Jonathan. He had the whole night planned out. Where they would eat...everything. He told her to rest up, so she could make it through a whole slow dance with him. He wasn't going to let her do anything else.

She accused him of being her doctor, but he was okay with that.

"Can you believe what God has done this year, Jonathan?"

"No, I can't. It's been the most exciting ride of my life. I can't wait to see what he's got up his sleeve for next year!"

40

Hannah and Drew came by the day of the prom to tell Sarah goodbye, and let her see Samuel one last time before leaving for home. They were one happy couple. They had fallen in love with Samuel and he was a great baby. Hannah proved to be a natural mother. Sarah didn't know when she would see Samuel again, but it didn't matter. She had done what she was called to do.

"Samuel," she told him, "you go out and change your generation. I'm going to be your greatest fan."

She hugged and kissed them all then went upstairs to get ready for the prom.

If you experience being raped whether by a stranger, a family member, a "friend", or a date you need to tell someone: the police, your parents, a counselor, your youth pastor, or pastor. If none of these seem to be an option then I have listed some information about some hotlines. They can help you get the help you need.

Hope for Healing.Org
Christian oriented hotline: 1-877-949-HELP
National Sexual Assault Hotline: 1-800-656-HOPE

Statistics about rape:
44% of victims are under the age of 18
80% are under the age of 30
Every 2 minutes, someone is assaulted
54% are not reported
97% of rapists are not jailed
One out of every 6 women are the victim of an attempted or completed rape
Most women know their attacker

Saying all this: if you are a child of God you do not need to walk in fear but wisdom. Put your trust in the Lord and let him order your steps and walk in them. Then you can claim Psalms 91 that "no evil will befall you and no plague will come near your dwelling place." "We wrestle not against flesh and blood, but against principalities, and wickedness in high places." That is why we need to walk with the armor of God on every day.

If you have been raped in your past and can't seem to break out of its bondage then you need to go to a Christian counselor and get some help. God wants you to walk in freedom and life. If God can take the "sting" out of death, then he can take the "sting" out your bad memories. It is my prayer, and God's that you walk in newness of life. Your church, or a local church can give you some names of Christian counselors in your vicinity.

Here are some other helpful contacts:
teenchallengeusa.com - for troubled teens
celebraterecovery.com - a Christian based recovery program from any type of addiction